South Africa

Travel with
**Insider
Tips**

How this Guide Works

Our guide introduces you to the sights in South Africa in six chapters. The map below presents an overview of how the chapters are arranged. Each one has been allocated a special colour. In order to help you plan your trip, we have subdivided all the main points of interest in each chapter into three sections: the must-see sights are listed under the *TOP 10* and also highlighted in the book with two stars. You'll find other important sites that didn't quite make our Top 10 list in the *Don't Miss* section. A selection of other places worth seeing appears in the *At Your Leisure* section.

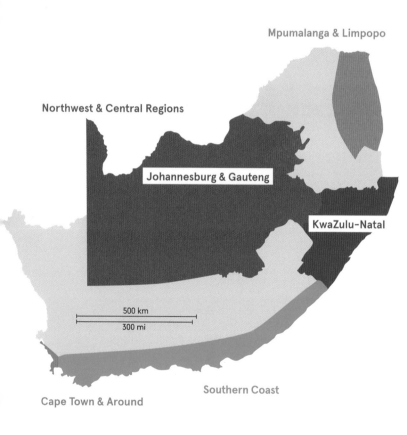

Mpumalanga & Limpopo

Northwest & Central Regions

Johannesburg & Gauteng

KwaZulu-Natal

500 km

300 mi

Southern Coast

Cape Town & Around

Northwest & Central Regions

Walks & Tours

Practicalities

Appendix

Magical Moments

Be in the right place at the right time and experience
magical moments you will never forget.

The manor house on the Zorgvliet wine estate in Stellenbosch dates back to 1624

Women in Oudtshoorn selling feather dusters made out of dyed ostrich feathers

★★ TOP 10

Not to be missed! Our top hits – from the absolute No. 1 to No. 10 – help you plan your tour of the most important sights.

❶ ★★ Kruger National Park
One of the largest reserves in the world offers unparalleled game drives through the wilderness – it is the country's premier park (p. 148).

❷ ★★ City Centre (Cape Town)
Known as the Mother City, it is often rated as one of the most beautiful cities in the world and it is where the cultural diversity of the Rainbow Nation is at its most colourful (p. 44).

❸ ★★ Garden Route
The southern coast between Cape Town and Port Elizabeth boasts numerous nature reserves, wonderful bathing beaches and some outstanding restaurants (p. 68).

❹ ★★ uKhahlamba-Drakensberg Park
The soaring "dragon mountain" peaks form the border with Lesotho. The area is popular for outdoor pursuits and is known as one of the most scenic landscapes in the country (p. 94).

❺ ★★ Pilanesberg National Park
Occupying an extinct volcano north of Sun City, this is a wonderful place to encounter many of the animals that have been relocated to the reserve (p. 170).

❻ ★★ Panorama Route
This route in Mpumalanga takes in some of the most dramatic scenery in the country. It winds through the Drakensberg escarpment – which drops off to afford some spectacular viewpoints – and includes the magnificent Blyde River Canyon (p. 151).

❼ ★★ Zululand & Maputaland
A region of lush rolling hills famed for its great warriors and, in the north vast wetlands – with forests, lakes and lagoons – border endless, pristine beaches with fine sand (p. 98).

❽ ★★ Pretoria
The capital of South Africa offers interesting museums and heritage sites including the impressive Victorian parliament buildings (p. 122).

❾ ★★ Soweto
Nobody knows exactly how many people live in South Africa's townships. A visit to Soweto is a must for anyone who wants to understand the country's history (p. 126).

❿ ★★ Durban
A city with an unmistakeably Indian feel, its wide sandy beaches and seaside promenade make it a popular summer holiday destination (p. 101).

That South Africa Feeling

Experience the country's unique flair and find out what makes South Africa tick – just like the South Africans themselves.

Braai and Beer

The South African *braai* (barbecue) is more than just cooking meat outdoors on an open fire; it is integral to the South African identity, a social part of every event, excursion or gathering. The word *braai* includes building the fire, stoking the embers, grilling the meat and the actual socializing. On weekends a *braai* will often start at noon with the preparation of the fragrant wood fire, once it is lit then it is time for the first cold beer. Next the meat is marinated (using a secret recipe) and the vegetables are either added to a cast-iron *potjie* pot or wrapped in foil and tossed in the embers. Another beer and then it is time for the meat and the spirals of *boerewors* (sausage) to be cooked to perfection over the bed of glowing embers. A *braai* is not just about eating, it is not just about a fire but rather it is about people and community – *braai* is a way of life.

Home is Where the Heart Is

Needless to say there are still townships in post-apartheid South Africa but the government has done a lot to maintain and improve them. There are now tarred roads, electricity supplies and sewer systems – entirely new settlements have emerged. However, many South Africans who have done well for themselves do not want to leave the townships. It is their home, the place of their youth, the place of their family and friends. So, along with makeshift shacks, you'll also see some spacious mansions with several luxury cars in the garage.

A Day at the Mall

There is a strong mall culture in South Africa and mall parking

The Drakensberg area is ideal for hiking – pictured here is the Tugela Valley

The Twelve Apostles rising up behind Camps Bay,
one of Cape Town's most expensive suburbs

Street art in Johannesburg's Soweto
(short for South Western Township)

lots are always full. A trip to the mall is often a family outing as malls offer more than just shops; this is where you can find everything your heart desires. And they are usually fully air-conditioned. The malls also function as entertainment centres, providing everything needed for a successful day out – a range of restaurants, inviting cafés, children's playgrounds as well as service firms such as hair-dressers, cinemas and even flea markets and picnic areas. Everyone takes their time, strolling along, browsing the shops and enjoying themselves in a safe environment – the actual shopping is not that important.

Sport Unites
South Africans are passionate about sport and the national rugby team – the Springboks – are one of the best in the world and the pride of the nation. If you don't have time to attend a stadium game, visit one of the many sports bars and watch the action with friends or the locals. Football and cricket are also hugely popular, for a long time cricket and rugby were white-dominated sports and football was predominantly black. After returning to the international sporting world after apartheid and the success of the World Cup in 2010 it seems that the *vuvuzelas* have blown away racial barriers and redefined sports for the Rainbow Nation.

Nature Reserves
In 1846, the Cape Colony passed the first Nature Conservation Act; a lot has happened since then. South Africans are proud of their many small nature reserves, which are just as popular as the world-famous national parks. They are enjoyed across society: school children learn about the flora and fauna, families have picnics, tough men test their 4×4s, bird-watchers are kept busy, and photographers wait for the ultimate wildlife shot.

Celebrating Faith
While church worship in the white community is a traditional, reserved affair, church services in the black community are vibrant and exuberant. Sunday is a holiday in the truest sense of the word, services are a joyous celebration with the choir singing rousing songs and the congregation joining in for the chorus – and visitors are always warmly welcomed.

Women travelling on the ferry to Robben Island,
with iconic Table Mountain as the backdrop

The Magazine

The Rainbow Nation welcomes you with captivating charm, breathtaking scenery and spectacular nature.

Pages 12–35

The mighty Table Mountain massif dominates Cape Town and the surrounding Atlantic Ocean – it is easily accessible by cable car and the panoramic views are exceptional

A World in One Country

South Africa's appeal lies in its natural beauty. It's also a melting pot of origins, cultures, languages and beliefs.

Western and Eastern Cape Provinces

The highlight of the Western Cape province is Cape Town. The city is home to a cosmopolitan ethnic mix including Cape Coloureds – a distinct community descended from Malay slaves, white colonists and the indigenous San and Khoi peoples. Other attractions in the province include the winelands, the Garden Route, and fine beaches. To the north of the province is the Karoo with its quirky 19th-century towns. The Eastern Cape is dominated by the Wild Coast, a largely rural and richly green region dotted with *kraals* (villages) of the Xhosa people and backed by swathes of beach.

KwaZulu-Natal and Gauteng

Durban and a string of resorts line the subtropical Indian Ocean coast of southern KwaZulu-Natal, while to the north is the iSimangaliso Wetland Park. Offshore, coral gardens teem with colourful marine life. The coast has a rich cultural heritage as the heartland of the Zulu people and home to an Indian community who first came to the region to work on sugar plantations. The province has superb game reserves and is home to more rhino than anywhere else in the world. Inland, the hilly KwaZulu-Natal Midlands, studded with the intriguing 19th-century battlefield sites, rise toward the uKhahlamba-Drakensberg Park. The park's San rock art sites are one of South Africa's greatest cultural treasures.

Gauteng is home to the rather staid capital Pretoria, as well as vibrant Johannesburg. Gauteng has thrown up a rare wealth of early hominid fossils, and its most important palaeontological sites are protected in a World Heritage Site (since 1999), known as the Cradle of Humankind. Johannesburg witnessed some of the most important events in the struggle against apartheid and you can meet the people in the lively townships and visit the excellent museums to find out more.

The North and Northwest

Mpumalanga and Limpopo contain the vast Kruger National Park and offer South Africa's best opportunities to see the Big Five. The northwest of South Africa, comprising the Free State, Northwest and Northern Cape provinces, is an arid region of sparsely populated farmland, giving way to the Kalahari grasslands in the north. There are a few game reserves worth the effort of getting to; Kimberley and Bloemfontein have interesting historical pasts, and Sun City is hidden in the bush of the adjacent Pilanesberg National Park.

A visit to a Xhosa *kraal*, with its traditional round huts, provides first hand experience of their rich culture and history

From Divided to United

South Africa's recent history has been overwhelmingly dominated by apartheid, which means "being apart" in Afrikaans. After apartheid ended, Nelson Mandela (1918–2013) proclaimed the country, "a rainbow nation at peace with itself and the world".

And does the new South Africa reflect this statement? When the weather is fine, some of the country's large cities – spruced up with a lot of modern chrome and glass designs – look like massive amusement parks where everyone seems to have only two goals: fun and consumerism. Is this what remains of the vision that Nelson Mandela had of the country in 1994? At his presidential address Mandela said: "We enter into a covenant that we shall build a society in which all South Africans, both black and white, will be able to walk tall, without fear in their hearts, assured of their inalienable right to human dignity – a rainbow nation at peace with itself and the world". Thus ended the apartheid chapter of the country's history – politically at least. All that remained was for Mandela's vision to move people's hearts.

Resistance...

...against the white minority began as far back as the 19th century. In 1912, black intellectuals and politically minded individuals founded the South African Native National Congress in Bloemfontein. Later, in 1923, the name was changed to the African National Congress (ANC). It was founded to fight against racism and ethnic rivalries, for the political rights of the black majority and the improvement of their living conditions. Not only were black people denied the right to vote, but from 1913 they also had to live exclusively in designated areas of townships and homelands. Up until the Second World War, the ANC, which was rather urban and medium-sized, was content with petitions, protests and meetings. After increasingly repressive apartheid laws were passed from 1948 onwards, the ANC responded with strikes, civil disobedience and protest marches. Its membership rose rapidly to more than 100,000. In 1955 several organizations joined forces with the ANC. They adopted the Freedom Charter for a non-racial, democratic South Africa, which remained the ANC's core policy document until the 1990s.

Tensions

There were also tensions within the ANC. The Pluralists demanded equal rights, while the Africanists, contrary to the policy of the ANC at the time, were striving for a South Africa free from white rule. In 1959, the Africanists split from the ANC and founded the Pan Africanist Congress (PAC). On 21 March 1960, the PAC called for a peaceful demonstration against the hated pass laws in front of the Sharpeville police station.

A new generation looking ahead to the future (on the Moses Mabhida Stadium viewing platform, Durban)

The police, feeling threatened, shot into the crowd and killed 69 demonstrators. The international community reacted with horror and outrage. Throughout the country, strikes and demonstrations took place, at the cost of more lives. The government reacted harshly. On 8 April 1960, they banned the ANC and the PAC, who then continued their work underground and in exile. Both parties formed military wings. The ANC's wing was Umkhonto we Sizwe (Spear of the Nation) headed by Mandela, who became the president of the ANC and leader of the movement. Although the organization completed a few spectacular attacks, it was nearly destroyed in 1963 when Nelson Mandela (who was arrested in 1962 and sentenced to five years imprisonment) was sentenced to life imprisonment for sabotage after warfare documents were found at the Umkhonto we Sizwe headquarters. Activists were imprisoned (often without trial) and many died in police custody. Executions reached record highs. When the government wanted to introduce Afrikaans (the language of the white oppressors) as the language of instruction in schools, 20,000 Soweto pupils demonstrated on 16 June 1976. The police responded with gunfire, killing two unarmed youths. There were bloody unrests all over the country. This time the government did not manage to

bring the situation under control again until the end of 1977. In 1977 the leader of the Black Consciousness Movement, Steve Biko, died in prison from injuries sustained during torture.

A Noble Peace Prize

In early 1990, president FW de Klerk (the "Gorbachev of Africa") went against his own party and the white far-right and legalized struggle organizations such as the ANC, the PAC and the Communist Party. He also released Nelson Mandela from prison and began negotiations to form a new transitional

On the right track? Mandela's vision continues to be both the county's challenge and its mission

government. For their efforts to end apartheid and lay the foundations for democracy, Mandela and de Klerk received the Nobel Peace Prize in 1992. Following South Africa's first free parliamentary elections in April 1994, the ANC emerged as the strongest party with 62 per cent of the vote. Nelson Mandela remained in office as president until 1999 and died on 5 December 2013 from a lung infection.

Mandela's Heirs

To date, the ANC has won all elections with an absolute majority. Despite this, none of Mandela's successors – neither the technocrat Thabo Mbeki (1999–2008) or his charismatic but highly controversial successor Jacob Zuma – have been able to bring peace to this divided society. Zuma survived several charges of corruption but was eventually forced by the ANC to resign in 2018. His successor, Cyril Ramaphosa, was deputy president under Zuma and is believed to be one of the richest men in South Africa. The unresolved question of land distribution – 72 per cent of the agricultural land is owned by whites – is at the top of his to-do list.

Game Plan

South Africa's diverse network of national parks and game reserves is certainly its main attraction. They encompass landscapes that include desert and forest, scrubland and coast, mountains and marine reefs – and each region guarantees exciting safari experiences. There's just one condition: you have to be up at dawn because that is when the game are at their most active.

Several South African reserves are home to the Big Five: lion, leopard, buffalo, rhino and elephant. This is a term that originally described the five animals most feared by professional hunters, and capturing this legendary quintet on camera is a prime goal of most modern photographic safaris. To bump up the Big Five to the Big Seven you need to add the great white shark and the southern right whale to the list, both species can be seen in the marine reserve section of the Addo Elephant National Park. Other interesting animals to photograph are cheetah, giraffe, hippo and zebra, and there is a range of other species

The preferred habitat of lions is grassy plains and open savannah

Springbok are found in southern Africa's open plains and grass savannahs

of mammals, reptiles and birds that deserve equal attention.

Many parks and reserves are run by government or provincial administrations, and are economical to visit by self-driving and staying in park chalets or campsites. Most offer additional guided game drives or walks. The increasing number of private game reserves is making a huge impact on the environment, and many of them are reintroducing animals in areas where they had previously become extinct. With a bigger budget, you can stay at these lavish all-inclusive game lodges or beautifully positioned tented camps for an unsurpassed wilderness experience. By the way, the "tents" on offer at the exclusive lodges are often luxurious suites with stylish décor and all the amenities.

When to Visit

In both the public and private parks and reserves, the main activity is game drives, which are best undertaken in the early morning or late afternoon when the animals are at their most active and make their way to waterholes and rivers. Spotlight safaris after dark offer the opportunity to spot nocturnal creatures. The climate varies around the country but as a rule of thumb the dry season, when the animals are concentrated around waterholes and the grass is short, is the best time for game viewing. The wet season does have its advantages as the animals will be in good condition after feeding on the new shoots and there's the opportunity to witness breeding or calving.

One lifetime would not be enough to discover all the natural wonders on offer in these parks; the social life of the elephants, the interplay between flowers and insects, the survival and the battle between the species, the ups and downs, the annual display of wild flowers in the seemingly barren soil, and the whales that make their way to the coast. Each climate zone in South Africa has its own wildlife and tells its own natural history. Even the arid Karoo has its own diverse animals and plants, although they are not as obvious as those in the tropical areas along the Indian Ocean, where the trees are dense with lush creepers and crocodiles bask in the sun. Botanists classified the Cape's rich and unique vegetation as the Cape Floral Kingdom, the smallest and most diverse of the world's six floral kingdoms. No less impressive are the bizarre succulents in the country's semidesert region.

Greater Kruger National Park
The provinces of Limpopo and Mpumalanga offer access to the Kruger National Park, which harbours more mammal species than any other sanctuary in Africa. A number of private reserves adjoin the Kruger, and now that fences have been taken down and animals can move freely between the park and the private reserves, the region is promoted as the Greater Kruger National Park. The Kruger is also a component of the Great Limpopo Transfrontier Park encompassing protected areas in Zimbabwe and Mozambique.

KwaZulu-Natal and Northwest Provinces
KwaZulu-Natal has the country's highest concentration of reserves, and these cover a wide variety of habitats. Hluhluwe-iMfolozi National Park is home to the largest concentration of rhino in the world, while the iSimangaliso Wetland Park harbours crocodiles and hippos. The little-visited waterlogged reserves along the Mozambique border have an array of wildlife from elephants to turtles. The uKhahlamba-Drakensberg Park offers unparalleled attractions for hikers and birdwatchers.

Northwest Province is home to the Pilanesberg National Park, an area of former farmland that has been restocked with animals from all around the country. The nearby Madikwe Game Reserve lies on a game transition zone on the edges of the Kalahari. Both are home to the Big Five.

The Cape Provinces
The Eastern Cape parks include the Mountain Zebra National Park and

Close encounters with elephant are a highlight for those on safari in Addo Elephant National Park (above); Breeding programmes aim to prevent the decline of cheetah populations and other critically endangered species (left); Hippos in the iSimangaliso Wetland Park in KwaZulu-Natal (right)

Addo Elephant National Park, while the coastal parks such as the Tsitsikamma are rich in marine life. Also in this province, private game reserves such as the critically acclaimed Shamwari and Kwandwe are re-establishing wildlife that hadn't been seen in the region for many years.

The Northern Cape is best known for the remote Kgalagadi Transfrontier National Park that stretches into neighbouring Botswana. Kgalagadi is home to hardy desert-adapted animals such as gemsbok and black-maned lions.

The Table Mountain National Park in the Western Cape is scenically beautiful and includes the mountain chain that stretches from Signal Hill to Cape Point along the Cape Peninsula.

Groot Constantia has been producing sought-after wines for over 200 years

---

Grape Expectations

After his arrival in Table Bay in 1652, the first Commander of the Cape, Jan van Riebeeck, planted the first vine – thought to have been a French Muscat. By 1659 he was able to write in his diary, "Today, so praise be to God, wine was pressed from Cape grapes for the first time".

So winemaking in South Africa took root. Commander Simon van der Stel, who succeeded Van Riebeeck, continued where his predecessor left off, establishing his own estate, Groot Constantia, in 1699. A group of Huguenot Protestants, already experienced winemakers, settled in South Africa in the 1680s, having fled persecution in their native France, and laid down the vines around Franschhoek (French Corner). Wines made here were much sought after in Europe, with Napoleon and Frederick the Great of Prussia among their admirers. In the early days, wine was produced for the benefit of the ships passing the Cape en route from Europe to the East Indies. Wine kept better than water on long sea voyages, and it was also believed that young red wine could stave off scurvy. Today a wide range of grape varieties are grown throughout the Western Cape and as far north as the Orange River Valley.

Fresh, Fruity, White

The top white wine grape is Chenin Blanc (also called Steen in South Africa) a variety that has its origins in the Loire Valley in France. Its naturally high acidity produces fresh, lively wines, but its share has declined by 40 per cent in recent decades. Currently in vogue are Colombard, Chardonnay and Sauvignon Blanc, rather rare is the "real" Riesling. Muscat d'Alexandrie (Hanepoot) is cultivated for fortified sweet wines while the Sultana variety is mainly used for table grapes and brandy.

Perfect Pinotage

South Africa has followed the trend towards the increased consumption of red wine. Production of international varieties has increased sharply but even Pinotage, a cross between Pinot Noir and Cinsaut/ Hermitage, which is unique to South Africa, has tripled its share. The best red wines are from Bordeaux grapes and include Cabernet Sauvignon, Shiraz, Merlot, Cinsaut, Cabernet Franc and Pinot Noir.

There is a global demand for South Africa's premium wines

Cape Wine Success

Up to a billion litres (220 million gallons) of wine is produced in South Africa every year on more than 600 wine estates. Most South African wines aren't labelled by region, but rather by grape variety and style. The grape itself, and the reputation of the winery that made the wine, are the two things to watch for – region is of lesser value. For something special at virtually no price at all, order a bottle of Cap Classique bubbly such as Krone from the Twee Jonge Gezellen estate.

Sporting Chance

South Africa is a sports mad country and fans, even those that aren't athletes, are passionate about supporting and watching the many sporting events that take place throughout the country all year round.

Football is the most popular sport in South Africa and each game is an incredibly loud spectacle, as visitors to the 2010 FIFA World Cup found out for themselves when they were surrounded by *vuvuzela*-blowing, cheering fans. This was the first time this global event was held on African soil. The national team, nicknamed Bafana Bafana (meaning "our boys") tends to perform quite erratically, though it did win the 1996 Africa Cup of Nations, and it has qualified three times for the FIFA World Cup; in 2018 they failed to qualify. The main domestic competition is the Premier Soccer League (www.safa.net).

Cyclists preparing for the start of the Cape Town Cycle Tour

Rugby is Number Two

The second most popular sport is rugby and in contrast to football fans, the stands at rugby matches are more subdued. The greatest moment in South African rugby (www.sarugby.co.za) came in 1995, when after years of being ostracized from world sport during apartheid, the Springboks hosted and won the Rugby World Cup, beating New Zealand's All Blacks 15–12. An excited Nelson Mandela presented the cup to the team's captain, Francois Pienaar, a white Afrikaner. Mandela donned the same "boks" green-and-gold number six jersey as Pienaar and the two embraced in a gesture of racial reconciliation that gladdened the hearts of South Africans everywhere.

Cricket is Number Three

Cricket (www.cricket.co.za) is the third most popular sport in South Africa. For more than 20 years during apartheid, South African cricket, like rugby, was largely isolated from the rest of the world. However, once the South African team, the Proteas, were allowed to play internationally again, the country soon established itself as one of the world's leading cricketing nations. South Africa hosted the World Cup in 2003, which, unfortunately for local fans, was won by Australia. The team currently holds the record for the highest successful run chase in a one-day international (438–9 in 49.5 overs) against Australia in 2006, considered by many to be the greatest one-day match ever to have been played.

A Land of Golfers

South Africa is also a land of golfers (www.saga.co.za). With its more than 500 courses, ideal climate and scenic charms, the country attracts players from all over the world. One of the most important events that draw world champions is the Nedbank Golf Challenge that takes place in December at Sun City (www.nedbankgolfchallenge.com). The classic South Africa tournament is the Sunshine Tour with the South African Open, the Dunhill Championship and the Joburg Open, which is held throughout the year mainly in South Africa, but also in Namibia, Zambia,

Sunday cricket training session in Cape Town

Swaziland and Zimbabwe (www. sunshinetour.com).

Cycling

The country is a great destination for cycling fans. The tough Cape Epic (www.cape-epic.com) is a major fixture on the international mountain bike calendar. It takes place late in the South African summer (March) and over 1,000 cyclists from all over the world come take part in this "Tour de France of mountain biking". Teams of two have eight days to complete the 800km (500mi) route with altitude climbs totalling 15,000m (49,200ft). The course route is changed yearly and is also open to amateurs. The Cape Town Cycle Tour circles the Cape Peninsula (www.cycletour.co.za) and is open to all amateurs. Every March, more than 35,000 participants cycle the 109km (68mi) route, making this one of the country's largest and most popular sporting events.

Runners Welcome

The Two Oceans Marathon (56km/35mi and 21km/13mi half marathon), which takes place on Easter Sunday and winds (with a 500m/1,640ft altitude climb) along the scenic Indian and Atlantic coasts of the Cape Peninsula. The popular marathon draws up to 15,000 participants. The Comrades Marathon in June follows a 90km

(56mi) route between Durban and Pietermaritzburg (the direction changes each year) and participants must complete the race in under twelve hours.

All Water Sports

South Africans love water and there is an incredible array of water sports and activities on offer. In February (with temperatures up to 40°C/104°F) you can tackle the Dusi Canoe Marathon on the Msunduzi River from Pietermaritzburg to Durban – one of the most prestigious canoe competitions in the world. It started in 1951 as a one day race but now takes place over three days when 2,000 participants paddle (and carry) their canoes a distance of 125km (77mi). The record time stands at eight hours. In July, Jeffrey's Bay (www. worldsurfleague.com) hosts the J-Bay Open, which attracts the world's top pro surfers. Breaks such as the famous Supertubes are legendary. The Midmar Mile (www.midmarmile.co.za) on the Midmar Dam near Pietermaritzburg has earned a World Record (2009) for the largest open water event; almost 14,000 swimmers completed that race. Since 2012 the National Open Water Swim Competition has been taking place in April on the Albert Falls Dam.

Right: Adventure sport in a setting of natural beauty: abseiling in the Featherbed Nature Reserve in Knysna, Western Cape

eGoli – Place of Gold

The province of Gauteng means "Place of Gold" in Sesotho, while the isiZulu name for its capital Johannesburg, eGoli, means "City of Gold".

The name is no coincidence; in 1886 the world's richest gold deposit was discovered on the Witwatersrand, 50km (30mi) from the capital of Pretoria. A reef 430km (267mi) long and 24km (15mi) wide was quickly identified, which instantly drew prospectors from across the globe. Before a year had passed, 20,000 people had settled on claims and by 1889 more than 19,600kg (630,000oz) of gold had been mined.

Birth of a New City
A shanty mining camp of wagons and tents called Ferreira's Town rapidly grew on the bare veld. The Pretoria government laid out a plan for a formal town immediately north of the main gold reef and named it Johannesburg after two government commissioners – Johannes Meyer and Johann Rissik.

A Golden Legacy
Today South Africa produces five per cent of the world's gold. About 95

Gold Reef City, the theme park on the grounds of Crown Mines, with its historic shaft, one of the richest and deepest the world

A reminder of Johannesburg's mining heritage: a toxic gold mine dump outside the city

per cent of the country's gold mines are underground, reaching depths of over 3.8km (2.35mi), the deepest gold mines in the world. Johannesburg's 3,293m-deep (10,800ft) Shaft No 14 opened in 1897 and closed in 1971, during which time it produced 1.4 million kg (3.08 million lb) of gold. Today the tourist attraction of Gold Reef City is based at the shaft where you can go underground to depths of 220m (722ft). This was the last operating mine in the city centre itself, but there are still 40 working gold mines in Gauteng and South Africa has enormous gold ore reserves, estimated at 6,000 tonnes. Today the classic view of Jo'burg – pale-yellow mine dumps in the foreground and skyscrapers in the background – will be retained, as while most dumps are being cleared for development, some are being preserved as a reminder of the history of a city founded on gold.

The Other George Harrison

In 1886 a sleepy farm on the Transvaal veld was rudely awakened when Australian miner George Harrison smashed a rock with his hoe and yelled "gold!". The area was pronounced open to diggings and drew prospectors from all over the globe. Strangely, Harrison who is believed to have sold his claim for only £10, left the area and was never heard from again.

The Rainbow Nation

First-time visitors to South Africa are often surprised by the country's linguistic diversity.

A Ndebele woman in her village in Mpumalanga; the Ndebele belong to the Nguni language group

Language and Identity

During the apartheid era, only English and Afrikaans were recognised as official languages. In 1976 the introduction of Afrikaans, as the language of instruction in schools, sparked the student uprisings in Soweto. This led to a wave of resistance and prepared the way for the end of apartheid. Today, there are a total of eleven official languages. In addition to Afrikaans (the mother tongue of most coloureds) and English (spoken by almost 40 per cent of whites and most Asians) there is also isiZulu, isiXhosa, Sepedi, Sesotho, Setswana, Xitsonga, siSwati, Tshivenda and isiNdebele.

Powerful isiZulu

South Africa's largest population group, the Zulu, are culturally and linguistically dominant in KwaZulu-Natal and Gauteng. About 11.5 million people, just under 23 per cent of the population, speak isiZulu as their first language. The second language is isiXhosa with 8 million speakers, which is about 16 per cent of the population.

Most South Africans speak more than one language, usually Afrikaans and English or either one of those and an indigenous language.

A Zulu healer (*sangoma*) in the DumaZulu Traditional Village

Afrikaans as Lingua Franca

Afrikaans emerged from the dialects of the Dutch immigrants who arrived in the 17th century. Through contact with African and Khoisan languages, German, English, French, Portuguese and Malay, new words were added and other words changed their meaning. This also applied to pronunciation, spelling and grammar. Afrikaans is spoken by roughly 7 million people, more than 80 per cent of coloureds and almost 60 per cent of whites.

Language Changes

Pidgin language, such as Afrikaans, develops as a means to communicate when there is a society made up of different language groups. A rather more idiosyncratic pidgin language is Fanagalo, based mostly on isiZulu, with a peppering of English, Dutch, Afrikaans and Portuguese words. This was spoken in the gold mines as communication between white supervisors and migrant African labourers from other regions of southern Africa. Tsotsi Taal, a mixture of Afrikaans, English and African words, was developed to communicate across different languages in the townships, and is sort of gangster rap – *tsotsi* means "thug", *taal* means "lingo" – and is commonly used in Kwaito music (South African rap).

San Culture

The San, also known as the Bushmen by the first European settlers in the Cape, are nomadic hunters and gatherers that once roamed southern Africa. They carried little more than what they wore on their backs, lived in caves and shelters and spoke a unique language using click consonants.

When the white colonization of South Africa began in the 17th century, the San (a collective term) had already had several waves of tribes invading their homeland. Every new invasion drove the San to retreat further into inhospitable areas. The San are now considered the descendants of the original population of southern Africa. Their extensive knowledge of the mysteries of nature has resulted in unique abilities, which enable them to survive even in the most arid lands. Men traditionally hunted with poison arrows and traps, while the women were responsible for gathering edible plants and bulbs.

A Dying Culture

Today, these fascinating people live on the margins of society, often beset by unemployment, alcoholism, tuberculosis or HIV/Aids. It seems that there is no longer any place for hunters and gatherers in our modern society. Some San manage to continue their traditional life at tourist lodges or in nature reserves. In this context, a pilot project has been started at !Xaus in the Kgalagadi Transfrontier National Park (www.xauslodge.co.za). The state has returned land to two of the local San communities who have built a tourist lodge that now provides them with a sustainable income. There is also a living museum village where visitors can see craft demonstrations.

Bow and Arrow Hunting

The San also demonstrate to tourists their hunting and tracking techniques and teach them about animal behaviour. They wear traditional clothing but only because it makes for a good photo opportunity.

However, a project such as this does play an important and

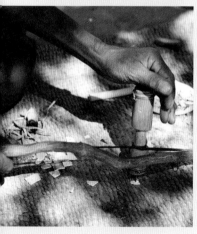

A San hunter demonstrates the ancient method of making a fire (above left); San are excellent trackers and hunters and use traditional weapons (above); San craftsmen skilfully creating ostrich eggshell jewellery (left)

valid role in San culture, as it is the only way that their knowledge, normally passed down through many generations in an oral tradition, is being preserved. This knowledge – especially their remarkable abilities as trackers – has even been used by researchers from the University of Cologne, and the Neanderthal Museum in Mettmann, to interpret the footprints and traces of early hunters in the remote caves of the Pyrenees in France.

A bird's eye view of Cape Town: Table Mountain and Lion's Head define the cityscape

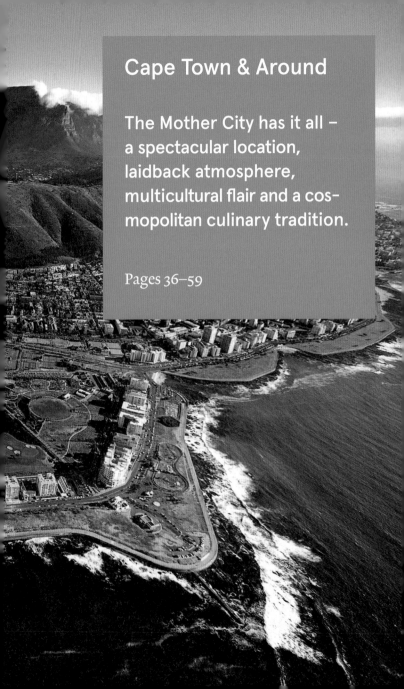

Cape Town & Around

The Mother City has it all –
a spectacular location,
laidback atmosphere,
multicultural flair and a cosmopolitan culinary tradition.

Pages 36–59

Getting Your Bearings

Hugging majestic Table Mountain and surrounded by the wild Atlantic Ocean, Cape Town is inarguably one of the most beautiful cities in the world. An absolute must is a sightseeing trip around the Cape Peninsula, with its magnificent beaches, and a tour of the scenic vineyards of the Winelands area.

Its unique location also makes Cape Town one of the most fascinating cities in the world. The heart of Cape Town is the City Bowl, which lies between Table Bay and the harbour to the north and the lower slopes of majestic Table Mountain (1,086m/3,562ft) to the south. The city has plenty of well preserved buildings and historic quarters that bear vivid testimony to its past. The refurbished Victoria & Alfred Waterfront is a great addition to the cityscape; once an unattractive harbour area, it is now a lively tourist and entertainment destination. The Bo-Kaap Malay quarter with its historic mosques, restored 18th-century houses and cobbled streets, stretches northwest of the city up the slopes of Signal Hill. South of Green Point the Atlantic stretch of coast has a string of attractive seaside suburbs from Sea Point to Hout Bay.

TOP 10
2 ★★ City Centre

Don't Miss
11 V&A Waterfront
12 Table Mountain
13 Robben Island

At Your Leisure
14 Kirstenbosch National Botanical Garden
15 Constantia
16 Cape Peninsula
17 Townships
18 West Coast

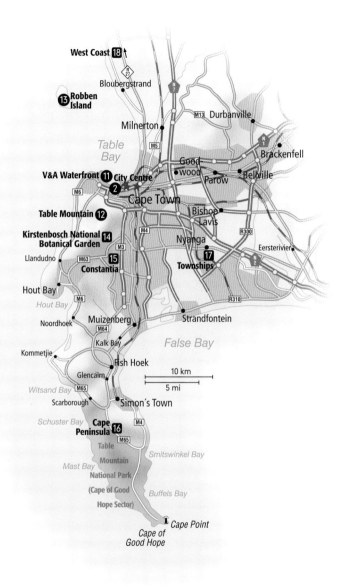

West Coast **18**

Bloubergstrand

13 Robben Island

Milnerton

Table Bay

M13 Durbanville

Goodwood

Parow Bellville

Brackenfell

V&A Waterfront **11** City Centre
2

Cape Town

Table Mountain **12**

Bishop Lavis

Kirstenbosch National Botanical Garden **14**

Nyanga

Eersterivier

Llandudno

15 Constantia

17 Townships

R300

R310

Hout Bay

Hout Bay M6

Noordhoek

Muizenberg M64

Strandfontein

Kalk Bay

False Bay

Kommetjie

Fish Hoek

10 km

5 mi

Glencairn

Witsand Bay M65

Scarborough

Simon's Town

Schuster Bay **Cape Peninsula 16** M4

M65

Table Mountain National Park (Cape of Good Hope Sector)

Mast Bay

Smitswinkel Bay

Buffels Bay

Cape Point

Cape of Good Hope

My Day
in Multi-coloured Bo-Kaap

The historic Cape Malay quarter is certainly one of the most picturesque areas of Cape Town due to its multitude of brightly painted single-storey cottages. It is best to do this tour on either a Tuesday, Wednesday or Thursday, as those are the days when the Malay cooking classes are available.

9:30am: Good Morning Bo-Kaap...

...or better, *goeie more*! Begin your day on Wale Street, one of the prettiest streets in the Malay quarter. Head for the Harvest Café (102 Wale Street; tel: 021 422 1199; https://harvest-capetown.business.site) for a delicious, healthy – and Cape Malay influenced – early breakfast. Sit outside on the rooftop terrace and watch as the neighbourhood around you awakens. You may want to try their legendary pumpkin fritters with Greek yoghurt, fresh berries and maple syrup. Locals say they are *lekker* but scrumptious is another good word to describe them!

10:30am: The Way to the Heart is Through the Stomach

Make a reservation with Zainie Misbach (www.bokaapcookingtour.co.za; cooking course R910) and meet her at the Rose Corner Café (46 Rose Street) to learn all her Cape Malay cooking secrets. After a thirty-minute walk through Bo-Kaap, you get down to business in Zainie's kitchen. For two hours you will

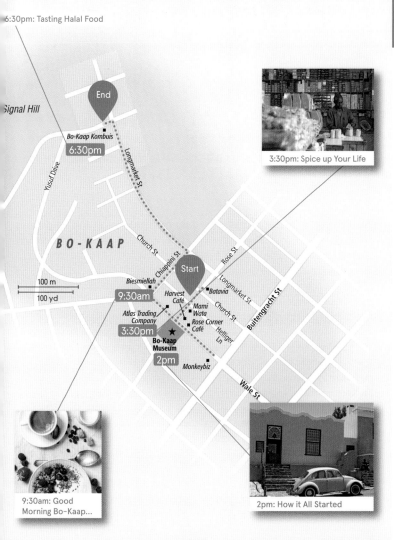

6:30pm: Tasting Halal Food

Signal Hill

End

Bo-Kaap Kombuis
6:30pm

Yusuf Drive

Longmarket St

3:30pm: Spice up Your Life

BO-KAAP

Church St

Chiappini St

Rose St

100 m
100 yd

Biesmiellah
9:30am

Start

Longmarket St

Batavia

Harvest
Café

Church St

Mami
Wata

Buitengracht St

Atlas Trading
Company
3:30pm

Rose Corner
Café

Helliger
Ln

★

Bo-Kaap
Museum
2pm

Monkeybiz

Wale St

9:30am: Good
Morning Bo-Kaap...

2pm: How it All Started

Above: The Bo-Kaap quarter with its brightly painted houses

learn how to prepare chicken curry, *samoosas* and *dhaaltjies*. Then you sit down to enjoy the food that you've prepared. Once lunch is over, and Zainie's happy with the result, she will present you with her masala mixture and recipe booklet.

2pm: How it All Started

The term "Malay" is actually misleading because most of the predecessors of the Cape Malays – who were classified as "coloured" under the apartheid regime – did not originally come from Malaysia. Their roots and what links and separates them, are explained in the Bo-Kaap Museum (71 Wale Street; www.iziko.org.za/museums/bo-kaap-museum; Mon–Sat 9–4;

R20) where you will also learn about the history and culture of the quarter and the how the Malays have left an indelible mark on the country through their cuisine.

3:30pm: Spice up Your Life

Now you have almost certainly developed a taste for the cuisine so next up is the Atlas Trading Company (104 Wale Street; www.atlastradingcompany.co.za) a spice shop where the air is full of the aromas of Asian spices. As you stroll through neighbourhood, with its streets lined by vibrant houses and mosques, you will also notice that the area is undergoing change. A number of new shops – such as Mami Wata (81 Rose Street; www.mami

3:30pm

3:30pm

6:30pm

Centre above: Vibrant community!
Centre below: Atlas Trading Company's spice bins
Right: Delicious food on every corner

wata.surf) a surf and clothing store, and Monkeybiz (61 Wale Street; www.monkeybiz.co.za) that sells trendy beadwork – herald the gentrification of Bo-Kaap. Batavia (114 Church Street; www.bataviacpt. co.za) is also a relatively new café. Sitting on a couch between all the kitsch and art, you will feel as if you are in the living room of a Cape Malay mama!

6:30pm: Tasting Halal Food
The inexpensive and tasty food served in Biesmiellah (2 Wale Street; www.biesmiellah.co.za) is halal, which means that it is prepared under Muslim dietary laws. No alcohol is served but there are great *lassis* to drink and authentic Cape Malay cuisine featuring *bobotie* and kingklip and mutton curry. If this restaurant is too basic for you, you can opt for the more elegant Bo-Kaap Kombuis (7 August Street, Schotsche Kloof; www.bo kaapkombuis.co.za) where the food is similarly authentic but served in a more sophisticated atmosphere, with a view of Table Mountain.

❷ ★★ City Centre

Don't Miss	Cape Town's city centre is vibrant and rich in history
Why	An exuberant, multicultural city with exciting museums
Time	One day
When	Any day of the week but almost all the museums are closed on Sundays
What Else	Allow time for some shopping
In Short	Diverse and cosmopolitan

Cape Town's city centre, known as the City Bowl, is bordered by Strand Street to the north, Orange Street to the south, and Buitengracht and Plein streets to the west and east. During the apartheid era Cape Town's residential areas were reserved for whites only; today visitors can enjoy the city's multicultural and cosmopolitan atmosphere.

The superb District Six Museum tells the story of the forced removal of 60,000 residents from the city's District Six from 1966. Once a diverse and mixed community, the apartheid planners razed the suburb. After the end of apartheid, some of the buildings were rebuilt. Displaced residents staff the museum and their own moving stories enhance the collection.

Built in 1679, the Slave Lodge provided very basic lodgings to slaves from the Dutch East India Company (VOC); up to 1,000 slaves were housed here in terrible conditions. There's a "Slave Code" on the wall – they had to go barefoot, couldn't sing or whistle, and were beaten if they stopped to talk on the street. The museum documents the colonial period, including the brutal suppression of the local population, the Dutch settlement and the establishment of Cape Town.

The oldest surviving stone building in South Africa, the Castle of Good Hope was built between 1666 and 1679. Today it houses a military museum, the William Fehr Collection (furniture from the 17th–19th century) and is the military headquarters of the provincial army. Martin Melck House houses an exhibition on the life of Nelson Mandela. The Bo-Kaap Museum depicts the lifestyle of a 19th-century Muslim family.

Other Places to Visit

The District Six Museum commemorates the many destinies changed by apartheid

South African National Gallery
✝ 232 B1 ✉ Government Ave ☎ 021 481 3970 ⊕ www.iziko.org.za
🕐 Daily 10–5 💲 R30

South African Jewish Museum
✝ 232 B1 ✉ 88 Hatfield St ☎ 021 465 1546 ⊕ www.sajewishmuseum.co.za
🕐 Sun–Thu 10–5, Fri 10–2 💲 R65, ID required!

INSIDER TIP Have tea and scones on the lawns inside the **castle** at the **De Goewerneur Restaurant.**

✝ 232 B2

District Six Museum
✝ 232 C1 ✉ 25 Buitenkant Street
☎ 021 466 7200
⊕ www.districtsix.co.za 🕐 Mon–Sat
9–4 💲 R40

Slave Lodge
✝ 232 C2 ✉ Adderley Street
☎ 021 467 7229 ⊕ www.iziko.org.za
🕐 Mon–Sat 10–5 💲 R30

Castle of Good Hope
✝ 232 C2 ✉ Buitenkant Street

☎ 021 405 1540
⊕ www.castleofgoodhope.co.za
🕐 Daily 9–3:30 💲 R20

Martin Melck House
✝ 232 B3 ✉ 96 Strand Street
☎ 021 405 1540 ⊕ www.capetown.
travel/products/martin-melck-house
🕐 Mon–Sat 9:30–5 💲 R40

Bo-Kaap Museum
✝ 232 B2 ✉ 71 Wale Street
☎ 021 481 3938
⊕ www.iziko.org.za
🕐 Mon–Sat 10–5 💲 R20

⓫ V&A Waterfront

Don't Miss	Entertainment hotspot for pleasure seekers
Why	For the lively restaurants, cafés and bars
Time	A few hours, or days...or as long as you want to!
When	At any time
What Else	The marine life in the Two Oceans Aquarium
Souvenir	Sunset photographs featuring Table Mountain

The regeneration of this harbour area in Cape Town has transformed it into a lively tourist and entertainment destination that is now a real enhancement of the urban landscape.

The main section is the Victoria Wharf, a giant shopping mall. In front of Victoria Wharf is the Union Castle Building housing the Iziko Maritime Centre, which showcases the maritime history of Table Bay. West from the Union Castle Building is the Time Ball Tower (1894). Beyond, the Two Oceans Aquarium focuses on the rich marine environment off the Cape coast. On the opposite side of Alfred Basin, and reached by a pedestrian swing bridge, is the Clock Tower Centre, with more shops and restaurants.

Atmospheric Waterfront restaurant with the silhouette of Table Mounta

INSIDER TIP There are over 80 restaurants, cafés, fast food joints and bars so you'll be spoilt for choice (R–RRR).

☩ 232 C5 ✉ Portswood Ridge
☎ 021 408 7600
🌐 www.waterfront.co.za
🕐 Daily 9–9

Iziko Maritime Centre
☩ 232 B5 ✉ Portswood Road
☎ 021 405 2880

🌐 www.iziko.org.za
🕐 Daily 10–5 💰 R20

Two Oceans Aquarium
☩ 232 B4 ✉ Dock Road
☎ 021 418 3823 🌐 www.aquarium.co.za
🕐 Daily 9:30–6, predator feeding at 3
💰 R165 (online R149)

⑫ Table Mountain

Don't Miss	The panoramic view over Cape Town makes it worth the effort
Why	The plateau has numerous fantastic viewpoints
Time	At least two hours
When	In clear weather
What Else	Selfies with cute little dassies
In Short	Cape Town is in a setting of unsurpassed beauty

Brooding, sentinel and ruggedly beautiful, Table Mountain offers spectacular views of the city and the sea, and it defines Cape Town.

To the indigenous nomadic people of the Cape, the Khoi, it was *hoeri kwaggo* meaning "mountain in the sea". It is named after the first man to climb it in 1503, the Portuguese explorer António de Saldanha, who named it *Taboa do Cabo* (Table of the Cape). You need not climb the towering 1,086m (3,562ft) mountain yourself, as there is a comfortable cableway up to its lofty heights. There are also several hiking paths, leading from the lower cable car station up to the top.

INSIDER TIP At the upper cable car station there is the **Table Mountain Café and WiFi Lounge.**

✛ 230 B3   ⓘ

Aerial Cableway
✉ Table Mountain Road ☎ 021 424 8181
🌐 www.tablemountain.net (online booking available)
🕑 Daily, first car up 8am, last car down 6–9:30pm, depending on season
🎟 R275–R295 (return)

Cape Town's Landmark

The iconic flat-topped mountain, built from massive layers of sandstone and slate, forms the northern end of the Cape Peninsula.

1

2   Camps Bay

5

3

Ben Schoeman Dock

Table Bay

❶ Table Mountain: At the summit is a self-service café serving meals, snacks and drinks, and a panoramic terrace with a network of short walkways (5 to 45 minutes) leading to vantage points offering fantastic views. On weekends, floodlights illuminate the mountain.

❷ Cableway: The Aerial Cableway has been in operation on Table Mountain since 1929. It was up-graded in 1997 and the new Swiss-made cable cars rotate 360 degrees during the journey. The cableway carries up to 2,500 visitors every day.

Alternatively, you can take one of the more than 300 hiking paths (of varying difficulty) up to the top. Depending on your starting point, the hike will take two to four hours.

❸ Devil's Peak, ❹ Lion's Head: Table Mountain is flanked by the 1,000m-high (3,000ft) Devil's Peak in the east – and separated by a wide valley – the 669m-high (2,200ft) Lion's Head in the west. Table Mountain continues south-wards as a wide plateau and descends steeply into Orange Kloof, which rises 200m (700ft) above sea level.

❺ Kirstenbosch: Table Mountain's position between the Atlantic and False Bay brings rain to its slopes and the southeast slope, where Kirstenbosch National Botanical

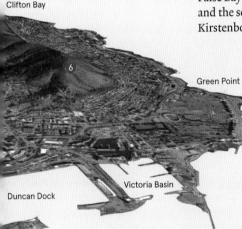

Clifton Bay

Green Point

Duncan Dock

Victoria Basin

Garden lies, has the highest rainfall (1,400mm per annum), the perfect climate for an extraordinary variety of plants to flourish.

❻ Signal Hill: The road winding up Signal Hill has the best views and is perfect for capturing shots of the city.

⓭ Robben Island

Don't Miss	Insights into the brutal apartheid system
Why	Maximum security building where Mandela was imprisoned
Time	Half a day
When	Only in good weather
What Else	View of Table Mountain from the island, a great photo opportunity
Souvenir	Deep respect for Nelson Mandela and his fellow political prisoners

The island has a history as a place of banishment. As far back as 1525 Portuguese sailors were believed to have abandoned a group of prisoners on the island and left them to die. It is

a UNESCO World Heritage Site, famed for the notorious B Section maximum security building, which was where Nelson Mandela was imprisoned until 1982.

Over 3,000 political prisoners were sent to the windswept isle during apartheid.

Victory for freedom: the guides on Robben Island were all previously political prisoners on the island

Conditions were harsh, yet when Nelson Mandela was finally granted freedom, he rejected recrimination in favour of reconciliation. He made history as the first black president of South Africa and even after his death he remains as *tata*, "the father of all South Africans", alive in the hearts of his countrymen. The island can only be visited as part of a guided tour. These depart from the Nelson Mandela Gateway and last three and a half hours (including boat ride).

INSIDER TIP ▶ Refreshments are available on the ferry and on the island.

ℹ️ ✝ 232 C5
✉️ Clock Tower, V&A Waterfront
☎ 021 413 4202

🌐 www.robben-island.org.za
⏱ Tours depart at 9, 11, 1, and 3 (in summer) 💰 R340

14 Kirstenbosch National Botanical
 Garden

The botanical garden on the eastern slope of Table Mountain is one of the most beautiful in the world. Cecil Rhodes bequeathed the area to the state in 1902. About 9,000 of the 24,000 indigenous South African plant species are cultivated on 40ha (100 acres) of the 528ha (1,304-acres) garden. Of historical interest are some wild almonds planted by Jan van Riebeeck in 1660, and an avenue of camphor and sycamore trees planted by Cecil Rhodes in 1898. The main flowering season is from mid-August to mid-October. From January to March the red disa orchid, called the Pride of Table Mountain, blooms along the garden's streams and shady ravines while the proteas display their colourful splendour from May to October. Special attractions include the Fragrance and Useful Plants gardens as well as the Protea and the Sculpture gardens. Colonel Bird's Bath – a pond built by Colonel Bird in 1811 – is bordered by the Cycad Amphitheatre, a collection of palm-like, rare and endangered cycads. The restaurant has a lovely shady terrace and in summer people like to picnic on the rolling lawns during the outdoor Sunday sunset concerts.

✚ 230 B3 ✉ 13km (8mi) southwest of the city centre off Rhodes Drive (M63)
☎ 021 799 8782 ⊕ www.sanbi.org
⏰ Sep–Mar daily 8–7; Apr–Aug 8–6 🗝 R65

Magical Moment

Spellbinding Table Mountain

Pack a picnic basket with tasty treats and a bottle of crisp white wine, and head up to the summit. Then find a calm, quiet spot away from the hustle and bustle around the cableway station. If you head in a southwesterly direction you will look out over the Twelve Apostles range, which winds along the Atlantic coastline. Drink a toast to being in such a beautiful end of the world!

15 Constantia

Nestled in the Constantia Valley is the oldest and most famous winery in South Africa, Groot Constantia. In 1685 the Dutch East India Company granted land to Governor Simon van der Stel, who built the gabled, whitewashed manor house and lived there from 1699 until his death in 1712. In 1791, as their wines became popular in Europe, the ground floor wine cellar was added and the vineyard was expanded. The manor house, with its valuable 18th and 19th century furniture, has been a museum since 1926. The estate offers wine tastings in the cellar; try to avoid weekends when Groot Constantia is very busy. The other prestigious estates on the Constantia Wine Route are also worth a visit – not only do they produce excellent wines, but they also have fine guest houses and/or restaurants.

> ✚ 230 B3 ✉ The estates are off Constantia Main Road (M41), 20km (12mi) south of Cape Town ☎ www.constantia valley.com ◷ Mon–Fri 9–5, Sat 10–1 (Groot Constantia, Constantia Uitsig and Steenberg also open Sun)
> **Groot Constantia** ☎ 021 794 5128
> **Klein Constantia** ☎ 021 794 5188
> **Buitenverwachting** ☎ 021 794 5190
> **Constantia Uitsig** ☎ 021 794 6500
> **Steenberg** ☎ 021 713 2211

16 Cape Peninsula

Cape Town lies at the northern end of a narrow, mountainous peninsula that extends southward for 60km (36mi) and is dotted with pretty coastal villages. Since 1998, two-thirds of the peninsula, including the southerly Cape of Good Hope Sector and the Boulders Beach penguin colony, has been protected within the fragmented Table Mountain National Park. The peninsula offers a succession of scenic highlights, but none matches the windswept vistas from Cape Point Lighthouse at its southernmost tip.

> ✚ 230 B2
> **Table Mountain National Park**
> ☎ 021 712 2337 ⊕ www.sanparks.org
> **Cape of Good Hope Sector**
> ◷ Oct–Mar 6–6; Apr–Sep 7–5 ✈ R135
> **Boulders Beach** ◷ Dec–Jan 7–7:30; Feb–Mar, Oct–Nov 8–6:30; Apr–Sep 8–5
> ✈ R70

17 Townships

Townships are still home to the majority of Cape Town's black residents. Visiting the townships is most safely done on a guided tour, as offered by the companies listed below. A typical tour will start off at Cape Town's District Six Museum (p. 44) before heading along the N2 highway and to the Cape Flats, where the townships spread east for approximately 30km (18mi) and house more than a million people.

> ✚ 230 B3
> **Cape Capers** ☎ 021 913 9553
> ⊕ www.tourcapers.co.za
> **African Eagle** ☎ 021 464 4266
> ⊕ www.daytours.co.za
> **Cape Rainbow** ☎ 021 551 5465
> ⊕ www.caperainbow.com

To this day traditional fishing methods are still in use in the Cape Peninsula, pictured here on Fish Hoek beach

18 West Coast

During September and October, it is well worth making the two-hour drive from Cape Town to see the thousands of indigenous flowers that carpet the valleys and nature reserves along the West Coast. For most of the year, the veld is dominated by a few perennial shrubs but in spring, more than 1,000 species of flowering plants emerge. The village of Darling, 72km (45mi) north of Cape Town, hosts an annual flower festival in September. Further north, 125km (77mi) from Cape Town, is the Langebaan Lagoon with four islets, which forms the West Coast National Park. The reserve covers and area of about 300km² (115mi²) and its unique and rich bird life makes it one of international importance. The vegetation is sparse, but in the spring, between August and October, the land is transformed into a spectacular sea of flowers.

✈ 230 A5
West Coast National Park
☎ 022 772 2144 ⊕ www.sanparks.org
🕐 Apr–Aug 7–6; Sep–Mar 7–7
🎫 R80 (R170 in flower season Aug/Sep)
Darling Tourist Information
✈ 230 B4 ✉ Pastorie Street
☎ 022 492 3361
⊕ www.darlingwildflowers.co.za

Where to...Stay

Expect to pay in high season per double room per night

R   under R1,500
RR   R1,500–R3,000
RRR over R3,000

The Backpack and Africa Travel Centre R
Cape Town's longest running upmarket backpackers' hostel is spread over three pleasant adjoining 19th-century houses with great views of Table Mountain. It is a popular place, so to avoid disappointment make reservations well in advance.

✈ 232 A2
✉ 74 New Church Street ☎ 021 423 4530
🌐 www.backpackers.co.za

Cape Grace RRR
This smart 5-star hotel is in a commanding position at the V&A Waterfront, with spacious luxurious rooms, modern African-theme décor, and superb dining at the One Waterfront restaurant. The Bascule Bar looks like a ship's galley and boasts the largest collection of whiskies in the southern hemisphere.

✈ 232 B4
✉ V&A Waterfront, West Quay Road
☎ 021 410 7100
🌐 www.capegrace.com

Cape Heritage RR
In historic Heritage Square where wine bars and restaurants huddle in restored 18th-century buildings complete with a still-operating blacksmith, this 4-star boutique hotel has 17 tasteful rooms and suites with historical features. Growing by the front door, and providing welcome shade in the courtyard, is reputedly the oldest vine in South Africa.

✈ 232 B3
✉ 90 Bree Street ☎ 021 424 4646
🌐 www.capeheritage.co.za

Daddy Longlegs R
If you are looking for an art hotel, this one has 13 rooms up a steep wooden staircase in a 1903 restored building in the heart of Long Street. All the rooms have been individually designed by Cape Town artists. They have minuscule bathrooms and not much furniture aside from a bed, but there's no denying their style.

✈ 232 B2
✉ 263 Long Street ☎ 021 422 3074
🌐 www.daddylonglegs.co.za

The Mount Nelson is one of Africa's best luxury hotels

Mount Nelson RRR
The Mount Nelson is Cape Town's famous Victorian colonial hotel built in 1899 and set in expansive grounds with a grand driveway lined with palms. About 200 rooms are in four individual accommodation wings, each with its own style of décor and private gardens. Facilities include a gym, two pools, tennis courts, two excellent restaurants and a 10-seater private kitchen where you can watch and talk to the chefs. You can visit for the sumptuous afternoon tea served on the terrace.

✈ 232 A1
✉ 76 Orange Street, Gardens
☎ 021 483 1000
🌐 www.mountnelson.co.za

De Waterkant RR
Choose from over 40 self-catering flats and cottages sleeping between 2 and 6 people, or Charles House and De Waterkant House, two stylish and intimate guest houses. These are scattered around the historic 18th-century quarter of Waterkant. Many have roof decks for great views, splash pools or pretty courtyards, and each is individually decorated.

✈ 232 B3
✉ 1 Loader Street ☎ 021 437 9706
🌐 www.dewaterkant.com

Where to...Eat and Drink

Expect to pay for a two-course meal per person excluding drinks:

R   under R200
RR   R200–R350
RRR   over R350

Baia RRR

This is one of the Waterfront's best spots for seafood with sweeping outdoor terraces and a sophisticated cocktail bar. The menu will tantalize your palate with tasty Mozambican shellfish, freshly caught Cape lobster, West Coast oysters or Norwegian salmon. For meat-lovers, there is a gourmet selection of grilled meat and poultry dishes. Linger at tables illuminated by the soft pink glow of hurricane lamps.

✛ 232 C5 ✉ Victoria Wharf, V&A Waterfront
☎ 021 421 0935 ⊕ www.baiarestaurant.co.za
◐ Daily noon–3, 7–11

Beluga RRR

You will find Beluga in the Foundry, a 100-year-old red brick building that used to be a metal works. It is a bistro-style restaurant that offers plenty of robust flavours, interesting ingredients and generous portions. Specialities include tender lamb shank, Belgian chocolate truffle cake and sushi. There's also a fashionable cocktail bar and a courtyard café where light meals are served.

✛ 232 B4 ✉ Prestwich Street, Green Point
☎ 021 418 2948 ⊕ www.beluga.co.za
◐ Daily noon–11

Grand Africa Café & Beach RR

This popular summer hotspot has a bar, restaurant and private beach. It is housed in an old warehouse and has a hip, lively vibe and extensive menu that caters to all tastes, from seafood through to pizzas and salads. Majestic views and beautiful sunsets make it the perfect sundowner destination.

✛ 232 B5 ✉ Haul Road, V&A Waterfront
☎ 021 4225 0551 ⊕ www.grandafrica.com
◐ Daily noon–11pm

Bukhara RRR

Elegant, fine-dining restaurant serving authentic North Indian dishes. The tandoori prawns and fluffy *naan* breads are delicious, and vegetarians will be in chickpea heaven. In fine weather you can sit outside on the veranda. There's another branch in the Grand West Casino.

✛ 232 B2 ✉ 33 Church Street
☎ 021 424 0000 ⊕ www.bukhara.com
◐ Daily noon–3, 6–11

Guests take centre stage in the cafés and restaurants

Café Mozart R

Pop into Café Mozart, just off Long Street, for a delicious full farmhouse breakfast with wonderful freshly squeezed juices. It's housed in a tall, narrow building between antiques shops and art galleries, and there are tables on the pavement. There are daily lunchtime specials and some decadent desserts. Try the home-made soups such as spicy pumpkin and gooseberry broth with a garlic roll.

✈ 232 B2
✉ 37 Church Street ☎ 021 424 3774
🌐 www.themozart.co.za
🕐 Mon–Fri 8–3:30, Sat 9–3

Chef Pon's Asian Kitchen RR

Chef Pon runs a buzzy, lively place with a long menu of affordable Chinese and Thai cuisine. Dishes that stand out include the hot-and-sour prawn soup, *tom yum kung*, crispy duck and Szechuan prawns. The food is simple, fragrant, generously portioned and is quickly delivered to your table. Make a reservation as it's a hugely popular choice.

✈ 232 B1
✉ 12 Mill Street, Gardens ☎ 021 465 5846
🌐 www.chefponsasiankitchen.co.za
🕐 Mon–Sat 5–10

The Codfather RRR

Treat yourself in this fine seafood restaurant where there are no menus and you choose a platter of fish, mussels, prawns, langoustine, crayfish and Portuguese sardines to be cooked to your liking and accompanied by stir-fried vegetables and a variety of sauces. Try the Namibian oysters or freshly made sushi topped with caviar – if you can't decide, the friendly waiting staff can recommend something.

✈ 230 B3
✉ 37 The Drive, Camps Bay
☎ 021 438 0782 🌐 www.codfather.co.za
🕐 Daily noon–late

Giovanni's R

The city's best deli, Giovanni's has a vast choice of Italian hams, cheeses and home-made pasta imported from Italy, while the shelves are filled with olive oils, balsamic vinegars, pickles, dried fruit and nuts, foie gras, truffles, fresh breads and pastries. There is a vast counter with freshly cooked ready meals and sandwiches sold by weight to eat in at the coffee bar or take away.

✈ 232 A4
✉ 103 Main Road, Green Point
☎ 021 434 6893
🕐 Daily 7:30am–8:30pm

Gold Restaurant RRR

Dinner starts off with a drumming session followed by a multi-course pan-African set menu, and the staff perform traditional dances throughout the night. It may come across as rather theatrical and touristy but the food definitely makes up for it – the feast is made up of 14 individual dishes and each one is delicious.

✈ 232 B4
✉ 15 Bennett Street ☎ 021 421 4653
🌐 www.goldrestaurant.co.za
🕐 Daily 6:30pm–midnight

Millers Thumb RR

Run by chef Solly, who cooks up a storm in the kitchen, and his wife Jane who reels off the menu in such a way it has you salivating, this Cape Town old favourite is set in a delightful house with three inter-leading rooms. Order Cajun and Creole dishes and look out for specials like seared tuna. The house speciality is Yaki Soba, a divine mix of chicken, prawns, stir-fried vegetables and fresh ginger in oyster and soy sauce.

✈ 232 A1
✉ 10b Kloofnek Road, Tamboerskloof
☎ 021 424 3838 🌐 www.millersthumb.co.za
🕐 Tue–Fri 12:30–2:30, Mon–Sat 6:30–10:30

Newport Market and Deli R

With a counter and stools overlooking the ocean at Mouille Point near the lighthouse, this deli is great for lunches and light snacks. It offers coffees, smoothies, excellent sand-wiches, salads and some hot dishes. The smoked salmon and cream cheese bagel is a firm favourite, or try the Cajun chicken wrap or lentil and barley soup.

✈ Off map at 232 A5
✉ 125 Beach Road, Mouille Point
☎ 021 439 1538 🌐 www.newportdeli.co.za
🕐 Daily 6:30am–7pm

Where to...Shop

Shops

The enormous shopping malls sell a wide range of items, with branches of the South African chain stores, as well as individual shops, restaurants, coffee shops and cinemas.

With its unique position, harbour atmosphere and well-kept historical buildings, the V&A Waterfront (Portswood Ridge; tel: 021 408 7600; www.waterfront.co.za) remains the most popular, and sells clothes, jewellery, African curios, gifts, books and market-style crafts at the Red Shed and Blue Shed.

The impressive Canal Walk on the N1 highway near Milnerton about 10km (6mi) north of the city (tel: 021 529 9699; www.canalwalk.co.za) is part of the Century City complex, and one of the largest shopping malls in the southern hemisphere. It houses more than 400 shops, restaurants, fast-food courts and cinemas.

Cavendish Square (Main Road, Claremont; tel: 021 657 5600; www.cavendish.co.za) is a smaller mall with fashionable shops geared towards the affluent middle-class residents of the southern suburbs. It's particularly good for clothing and has some great boutiques.

In the city centre Adderley Street has a full complement of chain stores and the Golden Acre Centre (www.golden-acre.co.za), while the red-bricked St George's Mall, the pedestrian zone between Castle and Adderley streets, has branches of the leading clothing chain stores and is peppered with informal stalls offering African artworks and curios.

Running parallel with St George's Mall is Cape Town's most eclectic shopping thoroughfare, Long Street, which gets quirkier and more bohemian as it leads closer towards Table Mountain. It has antiques shops (including the treasure trove of Long Street Antiques Arcade; 127 Long Street; www.theantiquearcade.co.za); new and used book shops; fashionable boutiques such as Mali South (96 Long Street; tel: 021 426 1519), selling clothing made from West African fabrics and craft shops, including the superlative Tribal Trends (72–4 Long Street; tel: 021 423 8008). In the nearby suburb of Observatory is the unique African Music Store (62 Lower Main Road, Observatory; tel: 084 308 3820; www.facebook.com/TheAfricanMusicStore), selling CDs from the Cape to Cairo and most places in between.

Elsewhere on the peninsula, Kalk Bay and Simon's Town are well known for their antiques and bric-a-brac shops.

Markets

There is an outdoor market in Greenmarket Square (between St George's Mall and Long Street; Mon–Sat, 9–4) selling African curios, jewellery, paintings, posters and clothes.

Colourful Green Market Square

The three-storey Pan African Market (76 Long Street; tel: 021 426 4478; Mon–Fri 9–5, Sat 9–3) sells items from all over the continent and you can also get your hair braided African-style or pick up an African snack.

Green Point Flea Market on Sundays, however, is the best place to find souvenirs (tel: 021 439 4805; 8:30–5). Hundreds of stands are set up in front of the stadium in Green Point selling wood carvings, ethnic jewellery and cloth, and a good selection of South African crafts. One lane is food, so you can grab a snack as you browse.

Elsewhere on the peninsula there's a Sunday craft market (www.bayharbour. co.za; Fri 5pm–9pm, Sat, Sun 9:30–4) at Hout Bay, which sells a decent selection of African curios, jewellery and clothes.

Where to…Go Out

Cinema
Cinema complexes are usually found in the shopping malls. The city's most atmospheric cinema is the four-screen Labia (68 Orange Street, Gardens; tel: 021 424 5927; www.labia. co.za). It tends to show more art-house, independent movies, with some foreign-language films.

Theatre and Concerts
The Cape Town Philharmonic Orchestra, opera and ballet troupes and imported musicals perform at Artscape (DF Malan Street, Foreshore; tel: 021 410 9800; www. artscape.co.za) or the Baxter Theatre (Main Road, Rondebosch; tel: 021 685 7880;

In summer the locals like to picnic during the Sunday evening concerts in the Kirstenbosch National Botanical Garden

South African jazz is earthy, reflecting its strong indigenous African roots

www.baxter.co.za): both have several theatres for plays.

Comedy and cabaret can be seen at Theatre on the Bay (1a Link St, Camps Bay; tel: 021 438 3301; www.pietertoerien.co.za).

The Fugard (corner of Harrington and Caledon streets, District Six; tel: 021 461 4554; www.thefugard.com), named after the renowned contemporary political play-wright Athol Fugard, hosts a varied selection of locally written productions.

There are sunset concerts at Kirstenbosch National Botanical Garden on Sunday eve-nings in summer. To find out what's on and get tickets, go to one of the Computicket offices in the shopping malls or visit www.computicket.co.za.

Nightlife

The trendy strip along Victoria Road in Camps Bay offers cocktails and sundowners in a sophisticated setting and is the place to see and be seen. The atmosphere is busy and boisterous and the strip attracts mainly a younger crowd. Word of warning, there are usually traffic jams along Camps Bay's beach promenade on weekends. People-watch at Café Caprice (37 Victoria Road; tel: 021 438 8315; www.cafecaprice.co.za; daily 9:30am–2am).

Mercury Live (43 De Villiers Street; tel: 021 461 1968) is a bar, disco and live music venue that is considered to be one of the city's best jam-session spots. It is always well attended and features performances by international guests as well as some of South Africa's best bands. See www.instagram.com/mercurylivect.

The top end of Somerset Road in Green Point offers a number of gay bars, and there are several trendy nightclubs here and in the Long Street area.

Right on Somerset Road is Beaulah (28 Somerset Road; tel: 021 418 5244, www.facebook.com/Beaulahbar; Tue–Sat 5pm–2/4am), a mainly lesbian bar and dance venue that welcomes everyone.

There is a great vibe and live music (jazz, funk, soul and blues) at The Piano Bar (47 Napier Street; tel: 021 418 1096; www.thepianobar.co.za; daily from 12:30pm), which serves good cocktails and delicious tapas.

Jazz fans should head over to the small and intimate Crypt Jazz Restaurant (1 Wale Street; tel: 079 683 4658, www.thecryptjazz.com; Tue–Sat 7pm–midnight). As the club is a popular live jazz venue serving tasty food, booking is advisable.

Outside of Cape Town is the West End Jazz Club (Cine 400 Building, College Road, Rylands; tel: 021 637 9132; Fri from 5pm until late) is highly regarded by serious jazz lovers. The venue attracts both local and interna-tional artists. No entry for persons under 21 years.

Also outside of the city is the Las Vegas-style Grand West Casino (1 Vanguard Drive, Goodwood; tel: 021 505 7777; www.suninternational.com/grandwest) with several nightlife venues and a vast gaming floor – the largest of its kind in southern Africa.

The bridge over the mouth of the Storms River in the
Tsitsikamma Section of Garden Route National Park

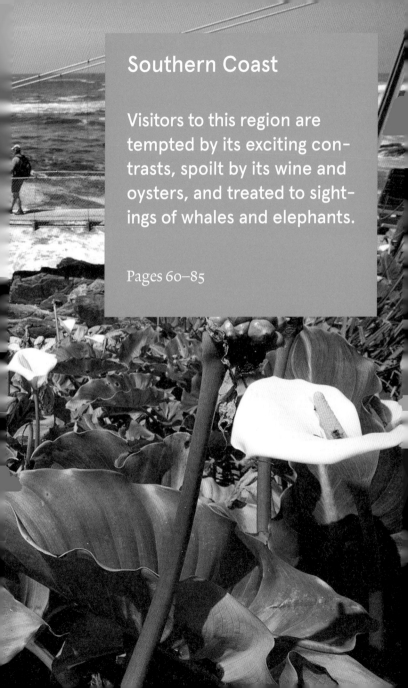

Southern Coast

Visitors to this region are tempted by its exciting contrasts, spoilt by its wine and oysters, and treated to sightings of whales and elephants.

Pages 60–85

Getting Your Bearings

After Cape Town the dramatic southern coast
of South Africa, which runs the entire length
of the Western and Eastern Cape provinces,
is the most visited region of South Africa.
It has a wide variety of landscapes, from indigenous
forests and swathes of wide beaches, to idyllic
vineyards and pretty country towns.

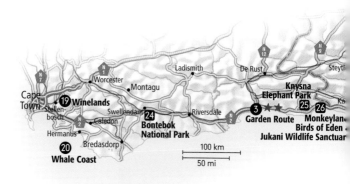

The region is linked from west to east by the N2 highway and the alternative Route 62. The tourist infrastructure is well developed and there are countless attractions and activities. The first port of call should be the impossibly scenic winelands that occupy the valleys from Stellenbosch to the Breede River. Southeast of Cape Town is the Whale Coast from where hump-back and southern right whales can be seen in the Atlantic in season. Then the celebrated Garden Route stretches to Port Elizabeth with its nature reserves and lush coastal forests. Worth visiting is the Addo Elephant National Park and, north-east of East London, the rural and ruggedly beautiful Wild Coast with its deserted coves, beaches and isolated seaside resorts.

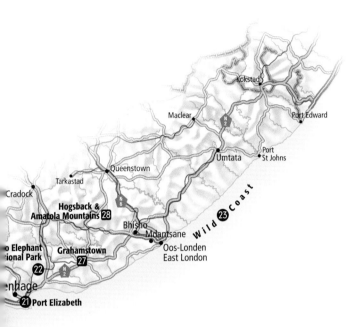

My Day
Hiking in a Forest

One of South Africa's most famous long-distance hiking routes, the Otter Trail, is a five-day hike through the Tsitsikamma National Park. The full hike may be too much for some, but the scenic first section of the trail is a fairly comfortable walk. After the hike head off for an exciting (pre-booked) Canopy Tour through the magnificent treetops of the indigenous rainforest.

9am: Waterside Breakfast

Start the day with a lavish breakfast of freshly baked bread and lagoon views at Île de Pain (The Boatshed; http://iledepain.co.za; closed Sun, Mon) on Knysna's Thesen Island. Afterwards head to the supermarket and stock up on drinks, sandwiches and fruit for your picnic. Now you can set off, take the N2 100km (62mi) east to the Storms River Mouth Rest Camp where you can buy your National Park ticket (R218) and collect a map of the hiking trail.

11am: All Along the Coast

From Sandy Bay, the boardwalk and path leads around bays and along the coast through the dense, evergreen forest to the mouth of the Storms River (Mouth Trail signposts). A number of paths lead down to the sea. The water may be too cold for a swim but if it is the season, you may spot a whale. After about 1,000m (half a mile) take a look at the Strandloper Cave where people sought refuge as long as 5,000 years ago.

2pm: Treetops From Above And Below

Storms River

Canopy Tour

2pm

1 km
0,5 mi

Kleinbos

N2

Storms River Adventures

← Knysna

9am

Start/End

Entrance Gate

Tsitsikamma National Park

Storms River

Storms River Mouth Rest Camp

Otter Trail

11am

11am: All Along the Coast

Strandloper Cave

Storms River

Hängebrücke

11:30am

Lookout

Mouth River Trail

Storms River Mouth

Viewpoint

Storms River Mouth Rest Camp

Storms River Mouth

200 m
200 mi

11:30am: Over the Bridge

Above and centre: Strap in and zip between the treetops on steel cables

11:30am: Over the Bridge

One of the many highlights is crossing over the Storms River on the 70m-long (230ft) suspension bridge. Look down and you might catch sight of canoeists paddling past. And then go left and follow the path (steep in parts) up towards the Lookout. After a climb of around 20 minutes, you will arrive at the first viewpoint overlooking the mouth of the river and the suspension bridge. A further 20 minutes and you will reach the next viewpoint 250m (820ft) above the breaking waves and overlook-

ing the coastline. It is now time for your picnic lunch, where you may be watched by some inquisitive dassies (rock hyraxes), before heading back along the same path to your starting point.

2pm: Treetops From Above And Below

After coffee in the National Park's restaurant, drive 15km (9.5mi) to Stormsriver Village, where the Stormsriver Adventures guides are ready to take you on the Canopy Tour that starts at around 2:30pm (stormsriveradventures.rezdy.

Above: There are always new bays and coves to discover
Right: End your eventful day with a delicious platter of fresh oysters

com/99778/tsitsikamma-canopy-tours; 3 hours R660). Securely latched with straps and karabiners, you glide through the forest on a network of steel cables between platforms. Soak up the scenery as you zip between the majestic crowns of indigenous stinkwoods, yellowwoods, hard pears and a gigantic Outeniqua yellowwood.

7pm: Fish of the Day
A farewell photograph with the friendly guides and then it's time to return to Knysna. At around 7pm, treat yourself to a delicious fish dinner at Fresh Line Fisheries (Railway Siding Dockyard; tel: 044 382 3131; www.freshlinefisheries. co.za). Very popular, so be sure to book in advance.

❸ ★★ Garden Route

Don't Miss	One of the most scenic (and famous) panoramic routes in South Africa
Why	Coastal forests, lagoons, seaside resorts and whales
Time	One to three days
When	At any time but try to avoid the busy summer holidays (Dec/Jan)
What Else	Variety of hiking and outdoor activities
In Short	Fascinating coastal landscapes

The Garden Route is a stretch of rugged coast with beautiful white sandy beaches, backed by a lush green hinterland. Its spectacular natural beauty has made it one of the most important tourist attractions in the country and a must-see destination.

The Garden Route (*Tuinroete* in Afrikaans) takes in a 220km (135mi) stretch of the N2 (2,200km/1,400mi), which follows the Indian Ocean coast from Cape Town to Swaziland. The Garden Route section between <u>Mossel Bay</u> in the west, and and the mouth of the <u>Storms River</u> in the east, is probably the most famous route in the country and it is particularly popular in December and January. Where possible you

Seagulls on one of the isolated beaches

should leave the N2, a section of the road is tolled, to explore some of the hidden places off the beaten track.

Mossel Bay is an attractive seaside resort and highlights include the Bartolomeu Dias Museum, which is actually a collection of museums – the Shell Museum, Maritime Museum and Aquarium. The Post Office Tree in the grounds was once used by early sailors to leave messages and you can still post a letter here today which gets a special frank. Although not on the coast, George has some interesting churches and an old slave tree where a lock and chain are

In Oudtshoorn you can enjoy an entertaining visit to an ostrich farm, where the ostrich races are a firm favourite

embedded in the trunk. North of George and through the dramatic Outeniqua Pass is Oudtshoorn, known for its many ostrich farms, such as the Cango Ostrich Show Farm, and the intriguing Cango Caves with their beautiful caverns of stalagmites and stalactites.

South of George is the picturesque village of Victoria Bay, set in a quaint cove with a safe swimming beach. The Wilderness Section of Garden Route National Park encompasses a network of rivers, lagoons and coastal forest, which is ideal for hiking or bird watching. Next is Knysna which is sheltered from the ocean by the Knysna Heads, a pair of rocky outcrops that form part of the Featherbed Nature Reserve.

Further along the coast, the seaside resort of Plettenberg Bay slopes downhill from a rocky peninsula overlooking great beaches – a good place for whale-watching. Robberg Peninsula Nature Reserve (R40) offers good cliff-top hiking on a rocky peninsula 6km (4mi) south of Plettenburg Bay, while you can take a cruise or paddle a canoe on the Keurbooms River. Worth a detour off the N2 is the sleepy village of Nature's Valley. Back on the N2, stop as it crosses the Bloukrans River Bridge, and if you dare, try the highest commercial bungee jump in the world at 216m (708ft). A little further on at

Storms River Bridge look down into the river gorge, and then spend some time hiking and enjoying the tremendous coastal and forest scenery in the **Tsitsikamma Section** of **Garden Route National Park**. The five-day **Otter Trail** runs westward

The ideal place for a rest stop on your hike

through the Tsitsikamma Section of Garden Route National Park. It's usually booked solid months in advance, but casual visitors can cover the trail's spectacular first leg as a round day hike from Storms River Mouth Restcamp.

INSIDER TIP There's no shortage of quality restaurants along the Garden Route. A must-do is to savour a dozen oysters with a glass of champagne with views over the lagoon at **Tapas & Oysters** (Thesen Island; tel: 044 382 7196; www.tapasknysna. co.za; daily 11–10; RR).

Mossel Bay Tourism
✛ 223 D1 ✉ Corner of Market and Church streets ☎ 044 691 2202
⊕ www.visitmosselbay.co.za
🕐 Mon–Fri 8–6, Sat 9–4, Sun 9–2

Bartolomeu Dias Museum
✛ 223 D1 ✉ Market Street, Mossel Bay ☎ 044 691 1067
⊕ www.diasmuseum.co.za
🕐 Mon–Fri 9–4:45, Sat, Sun 9–3:45
💰 R20

Cango Ostrich Show Farm
✛ 223 D2 ✉ 14km/8.5mi on the road to the Cango Caves, Oudtshoorn
☎ 044 272 46 23
⊕ www.cangoostrich.co.za
🕐 Daily 8–4:30 💰 R110

Cango Caves
✛ 223 D2 ✉ R328 near Oudtshoorn
☎ 044 272 7410
⊕ www.cango-caves.co.za
🕐 Tours daily 9–4 every hour
💰 R110/R165 (depending on tour)

Garden Route National Park (Wilderness Section)
✛ 223 D2 ☎ 044 877 1197 ⊕ www.sanparks.org 🕐 Daily 7–6 💰 R130

Knysna Tourism
✛ 223 D1 ✉ 40 Main Street
☎ 044 382 5510 ⊕ www.visitknysna.co.za
🕐 Mon–Fri 8–5, Sat 8:30–1

Plettenberg Bay Tourism
✛ 223 E1 ✉ Main Street ☎ 044 533 4065
⊕ www.plett-tourism.co.za
🕐 Mon–Fri 9–5, Sat 9–1

Bloukrans Bungee Jump
✛ 223 E1 ✉ 40km (25mi) east of Plettenberg Bay on the N2
☎ 042 281 1458 ⊕ www.faceadrenalin.com 🕐 Daily 9–5 💰 R990

Garden Route National Park (Tsitsikamma Section)
✛ 223 E1–2 ☎ 042 281 1607
⊕ www.sanparks.org
🕐 Daily 7–6 💰 R216

⓭ Winelands

The scenic Cape Wineland region has all the ingredients for producing excellent quality wines: well-drained, rather poor soil, warm, dry summers and cool winters. As far as the eye can see there are lush vineyards dotted with whitewashed Cape Dutch homesteads set against a backdrop of craggy mountains. The wine estates have names such as La Dauphine or La Provence, reflecting the French heritage of the settlers who brought viticulture to the Cape.

More than a dozen well-signposted wine routes link those estates that are open to the public. Most of the estates lie in picturesque countryside and wine tasting takes place in superb manor houses or atmospheric, cool wine cellars next to the vines. At some, port, brandy and cheese are also on offer. Also stop in the regional towns where you will see

The fertile Zorgvliet Estate in the picturesque Banhoek Valley near Stellenbosch

Ntsiki Biyela, the owner of Aslina Wines, was also previously named Woman Winemaker of the Year

splendidly restored Cape Dutch, Georgian and Victorian buildings, and you can browse in the many arts and craft shops and galleries.

Established in 1679, Stellenbosch is the oldest town in South Africa, and Dorp Street has a number of historic buildings. Some can be visited and have been restored and furnished in the style of their particular period.

Paarl (Afrikaans for "pearl") is named after the huge granite dome that overshadows the town and appears shiny like a pearl after rain. The town was established in 1720 and there are several historic buildings on the Main Street. The beautiful wine estate of Laborie is today home to the KWV cellar complex, which at 22ha (54 acres) is the largest wine cellar in the world. Franschhoek was founded in 1688 on land granted to the Huguenots and today is frequently dubbed the "Gastronomic capital of South Africa" with several superb restaurants to choose from. The Franschhoek Valley is where some of the Cape's most beautiful homesteads are found. The Franschoek Wine Tram is a vintage style hop-on, hop-off tram service to a variety of wine farms, such as Plaisir de Merle and Leopards Leap. It runs on six lines to the valley's vineyards (http://winetram.co.za).

The Drakenstein Lion Park is a sanctuary for captive bred lions that cannot be rehabilitated to the wild. Watching the lions at feeding time (Mon, Wed and Fri 4pm) is interesting for both young and old.

---

i ✠ 230 C3

Stellenbosch Tourist Office
✉ 36 Market Street ☎ 021 883 3584
🌐 www.stellenbosch.travel
🕐 Mon–Fri 8–5, Sat 9–2, Sun 9–1

Paarl Tourist Office
✉ 216 Main Road ☎ 021 872 4842
🌐 www.paarlonline.com
🕐 Mon–Fri 8:30–5, Sat, Sun 10–1

Drakenstein Lion Park
✉ Old Paarl Road, Paarl ☎ 021 863 3290
🌐 www.lionrescue.org.za
🕐 9:30–4:30 ✦ R60

Franschhoek Tourist Office
✉ 62 Huguenot Road ☎ 021 876 2861
🌐 www.franschhoek.org.za
🕐 Mon–Fri 8–5, Sat 9–5, Sun 9–4

⓴ Whale Coast

Don't Miss	Sightings of the world's largest mammals
Why	Whale-watching and penguin colonies
Time	Two to three days
When	In the South African spring or winter
What Else	Some of the best seafood restaurants in the country
Souvenir	Be sure to read *The Whale Caller*, a novel by Zakes Mda

From June to November whales visit the shores of South Africa, between False Bay and Cape Agulhas, on their migration route from the Antarctica. They return each year to mate and calve, making this the ideal coast for whale-watching.

From Cape Town follow the N2 to Somerset West and then follow the R44, and then the R43 around the rocky coast. From this route, there are some spectacular mountain and ocean views; on the way stop in Gordon's Bay for its fine swathe of beach and at Betty's Bay to see the colony of African penguins at Stoney Point.

The attractive town of Hermanus lines the sheltered Walker Bay, and these warm waters attract female southern right whales to calve and nurse their young. Mothers with calves can often be spotted from the cliff-top paths. The town's harbour has some restored fisherman's cottages and fishing boats, and to the south of the town are some good beaches. In late September, the arrival of the whales is celebrated with the Whale Festival (http://hermanuswhalefestival.co.za). In season Hermanus has its own tradition of a Whale Crier, who keeps watch from the cliff top and announces sightings by blowing his horn. It also lets the tourists know that it is a good time to set out on a whale-watching boat tour.

Mussels straight from the sea to the table at Fishermans Cottage, Hermanus

At Hermanus the cliffs drop steeply into the ocean, and the whales in the waters below seem close enough to touch

Further around the coast is <u>Stanford</u>, a Victorian village set on the picturesque Klein River, and the busy fishing harbour of <u>Gansbaai</u> where thrill-seeking daredevils can go on a shark cage diving trip. Off the coast are <u>Dyer Island</u>, a breeding spot for African penguins, and <u>Geyser Rock</u> where there's a Cape fur seal colony. Both are prized morsels for hungry sharks, and great white sharks patrol the stretch of ocean between the rock and the island, known as Shark Alley.

Further east at the end of the R319 is the <u>Agulhas National Park</u>, in which <u>Cape Agulhas</u> is the southernmost point of Africa.

INSIDER TIP If whales are in Walker Bay than grab a table on the rocks next to the ocean at **Bientang's Cave.** You won't get a closer view unless you are on a boat.

 ✝ 222 B1

Hermanus Tourist Office
✝ 231 D2
✉ Old Station building, Mitchell Street
☎ 028 312 2629
🌐 www.hermanustourism.info
🕐 Mon–Fri 8–5, Sat 9–3

Dyer Island Cruises
✝ 231 D1 ✉ Kleinbaai Harbour
☎ 082 801 8014
🌐 www.whalewatchsa.com 🦈 R1,200

Shark Cage Diving
✝ 231 D1 ✉ Gaansbaai ☎ 082 559 6858
🌐 www.sharkcagediving.co.za
🦈 R1,850)

㉑ Port Elizabeth

Port Elizabeth, dubbed PE by its residents, is the largest coastal town between Cape Town and Durban. Along with Uitenhage, Despatch and Coega, it forms part of the Nelson Mandela Bay Metropolitan Municipality, nicknamed the "Detroit of South Africa".

Culturally, Port Elizabeth is on par with the other large cities in the country; there is a thriving student scene with plenty of lively pubs and bars. Its long beaches also make it a popular holiday destination. The small town centre, with the Donkin Street Houses, the grassy Donkin Reserve and City Hall (1858) on Market Square, offers an appealing image of historic PE.

INSIDER TIP Enjoy calamari at **Die Walskipper** in Jeffrey's Bay.

✛ 223 F1

Nelson Mandela Bay Tourism
✉ Donkin Lighthouse, Belmont Terrace
☎ 041 585 8884 ⊕ www.nmbt.co.za
🕐 Mon–Fri 8–4:30

The Port
Elizabeth
City Hall

㉒ Addo Elephant National Park

Don't Miss	The chance to get up close to elephants
Why	Not only elephants, but also the Big Seven
Time	One to three days
When	In the dry season (June–September), when the animals gather around the waterholes
What Else	Wild dogs and black rhinos in the neighbouring reserves
In Short	Sundowners as elephants stroll by your lodge

When the third largest South African national park was established in the Sunday River region of the Eastern Cape in 1931, there were only eleven elephants living there, today the park is home to 600 elephants as well as herds of buffaloes and numerous lions.

The park is proud to be the only one in the world where visitors can see the Big Seven, which includes the Big Five

on the mainland, and the great white shark and southern right whale in the sea off the coast. You can visit the elephant section for the day or stay overnight in chalets, which overlook a well-trodden path to the waterhole. Seeing herds over 100-strong is a magnificent experience. Don't bring citrus fruits into Addo as the elephants have developed a craving for them.

Elephants at a waterhole in Addo Elephant National Park

From Port Elizabeth you can also visit a few other private wildlife reserves. Shamwari Game Reserve is a success story where the bush has been repopulated with animals not seen in this region since the 19th century. You can stay in one of seven luxurious lodges. The Amakhala Game Reserve has eleven luxury lodges and bush camps. The bordering

Magical Moment

An Inconspicuous Hero

Dung beetles have the right of way? Indeed they do and in Addo the road sign warn that these rare little bugs are protected. So when you spot one, stop your car and watch as they struggle to roll their large balls of elephant dung: it is heading off to bury its treasure. And in so doing, it will set in motion a new cycle of life by fertilizing the soil with plant fibre and planting new life with the undigested seeds. An indispensable hero of nature – the humble dung beetle!

Kwandwe Game Reserve is studded with four exclusive 5-star lodges while Lalibela Game Reserve boasts five game lodges.

INSIDER TIP You can eat at Addo's restaurant or cook your own food on your patio **barbecue** while watching elephants pass by.

✠ 223 F2

Addo Elephant National Park
✉ Off the R335, 72km (45mi) northeast of Port Elizabeth
☎ 042 233 8600
🌐 www.sanparks.org 🕐 7–7
🎫 R272

Amakhala Game Reserve
✉ 63km (39mi) east of Port Elizabeth ☎ 041 502 9400
🌐 www.amakhala.co.za
🕐 May–Aug 11–6; Sep–Apr noon–6
🎫 R1,050

Kwandwe Game Reserve
✉ 160km (96mi) northeast from Port Elizabeth on the R67
☎ 046 603 3400 🌐 www.kwandwe.com
ℹ No day visitors

Lalibela Game Reserve
✉ 64km (40mi) east of Port Elizabeth
☎ 041 581 8170 🌐 www.lalibela.net
ℹ No day visitors

Shamwari Game Reserve
✉ 72km (45mi) east of Port Elizabeth
☎ 042 203 1111 🌐 www.shamwari.com
ℹ No day visitors to the reserve

㉓ Wild Coast

Don't Miss	Remote and untamed coastal landscape
Why	Rocky cliffs, bays and a gently rolling hinterland dotted with Xhosa villages
Time	One day
When	Best in summer, as the climate in winter can be harsh
What Else	Nelson Mandela's home village
In Short	A glimpse into a former homeland

The Wild Coast is a land-scape characterised by isolated beaches – where waterfalls tumble directly into the sea – rugged cliffs and a hinterland of rolling green pastures. Formerly known as the Transkei, this is the homeland of the Xhosa people and it is where many of them still live in traditional *kraals*, which are settlements of round huts. It is also the birthplace of Nelson Mandela.

The Wild Coast remains unspoiled and rural – pictured here is Cintsa's peaceful beach

The dramatic Wild Coast stretches 280km (174mi) from East London to Port Edward in KwaZulu-Natal. It's urban gateway is the largely industrial and drab city of East London (which does have some good surfing beaches) don't dwell for long, but head northeast along the N2 to the coastal resorts. A short distance beyond East London you can go on a guided game drive to see elephant, giraffe, zebra, rhino and antelope in the Inkwenkwezi Game Reserve. Cintsa overlooks forested dunes and lagoons, while the isolated hotels in the beautiful bays at Haga-Haga, Morgan's Bay, Kei Mouth, Qolora Mouth, Nxaxo Mouth, Mazeppa Bay and Qora Mouth offer fishing, shell collecting, hiking along the cliff tops and endless near-deserted beaches. At Coffee Bay, named after a ship that ran aground with a cargo of coffee beans in the 1860s, visit the Hole in the Wall, where huge waves crash through a hole in the cliff eroded by the sea. Port St Johns further north lies in a lush, hilly, steamy forest where a couple of nature reserves are home to small mammals.

Inland and back on the N2, stop in Umtata (Mthatha), the former capital of the defunct Transkei homeland, to visit the Nelson Mandela Museum, which focuses on the life of the

formidable man. The museum is in two sections: the main section is housed in Mthatha's former parliamentary building and documents Nelson *Mandela's Long Walk to Freedom* (the title of his autobiography) and the staggering number of gifts he received from around the world. The other section is his primary school at Qunu 32km (20mi) west of Mthatha where Mandela grew up, and you can also spend the night here.

INSIDER TIP On Sundays, don't miss the buffet lunch at the restaurant in the **Inkwenkwezi Game Reserve** (noon–4pm; RR).

---

224 C2–225 D3

Inkwenkwezi Game Reserve
✉ 33km (20mi) northeast from East London ☎ 043 734 3234
⊕ http://eastlondon-info.co.za
◑ Daily 7:30–5
✈ Hiking tours: R250; safaris: R800

Nelson Mandela Museum   ⓘ
224 C3
✉ Nelson Mandela Drive and Owen Street, Umtata (Mthatha)
☎ 047 532 5110
⊕ www.nelsonmandelamuseum.org.za
◑ Mon–Fri 9–4, Sat 9–3, Sun 9–1
✈ Free, donations encouraged

At Your Leisure

24 Bontebok National Park

The original habitat of the bontebok antelope was the 56km (35mi) wide plain between Bot River in the west and Mossel Bay in the east. Up until the end of the 18th century, large herds grazed there but they were hunted to near extinction and by the 19th century their numbers had dwindled to 17. This small park was established in order to protect these remaining animals. Lang Elsie's Kraal – once a camp of the indigenous Khoi – is an excellent place to watch them. The park is also home to grey rhebok, Cape mountain zebra, duikers as well as more than 200 bird species. The area is covered in rare *fynbos* (indigenous heathland) and in the spring over 470 plant species put on a lovely floral display. You can see the fascinating wildlife as you drive through the park but there are also three short hiking trails.

✛ 222 C1 ✉ Off the N2, 6km (4mi) southeast of Swellendam
☎ 028 514 2735 ⊕ www.sanparks.org
⏱ Oct–Apr 7–7; May–Sep 7–6 ✦ R112

A bontebok antelope

25 Knysna Elephant Park

To get up close and personal with an elephant is a marvellous experience. Knysna Elephant Park has 12 tame elephants in the small park and offers one-hour tours to meet, touch, feed and interact with them. Guides give out plenty of interesting elephant-related information. The park has a six-bedroom lodge overlooking the elephants' night *boma* (enclosure) so you can fall asleep to the sounds of them communicating.

✛ 223 E1
✉ On the N2 20km (12mi) east of Knysna
☎ 044 532 7732
⊕ www.knysnaelephantpark.co.za
⏱ 8:30–4:30; tours every hour on the half hour ✦ R275

26 Monkeyland, Birds of Eden & Jukani Wildlife Sanctuary

Monkeyland harbours primates from all over the world, most of which are rescued pets. You can go on a guided walk through a wonderfully lush tract of tropical forest to spot the creatures swinging through the trees. A 118m (387ft) rope bridge spans a deep valley and allows views into the upper reaches of the forest canopy where some of the animals spend their lives. Next door, the Birds of Eden, a free-flight aviary housed in a 2.3ha (5.7-acre) mesh dome, spans more of the forest with a network of boardwalks; periodically a clever irrigation system sets off a mock thunderstorm with lifelike sounds. There are macaws, parrots, hornbills and sunbirds to name but a few. Just 10km (6mi) west is <u>Jukani Wildlife Sanctuary</u>, home to all kinds of big cats, not just those from Africa.

The Amatola Mountains are a popular destination for hikers

✚ 223 E1
✉ Off the N2, 16km (10mi) east of Plettenberg Bay ☎ 044 534 8906
⊕ www.monkeyland.co.za; www.bird sofeden.co.za; www.jukani.co.za
➊ Daily 8–5 ✦ R230–R260 per attraction; combined ticket: R450–R520

27 Grahamstown/Makana

Grahamstown and surrounding areas form part of the Makana Municipality. Dominated by Rhodes University, it has some wonderful historical architecture dating back to the 1830s when the town was established by British settlers. There are some fine buildings along the High Street and around Church Square. Leisurely wander around the impressive museums, churches, monuments and libraries in streets that retain a distinctively English air. Grahamstown is also the location of the annual National Arts Festival, South Africa's most prominent festival, which attracts over 50,000 people to the city every July.

✚ 224 B1
Makana Tourism
✉ 63 High Street ☎ 046 622 3241
⊕ www.grahamstown.co.za
➊ Mon–Fri 8:30–4:30

28 Hogsback & Amatola Mountains

A one-hour drive north of Grahamstown in the heart of the Amatola Mountains is the delightful village of Hogsback. Named after one of the mountains that supposedly resembles the back of a hog, this beautiful region has excellent hiking through rolling hills, hardwood forests and past misty waterfalls. Hogsback itself is a laid-back little place with tea gardens and craft shops strung out along the main road. The local people sell country fare such as jam and hearty soups, and you can pick up booklets detailing hikes in the region.

✚ 224 B2
Hogsback Tourism
✉ Main Road ☎ 045 962 1245
⊕ www.hogsback.com
➊ Mon–Sat 10–4, Sun 9–3

Where to…Stay

Expect to pay in high season per double room per night

R under R1,500
RR R1,500–R3,000
RRR over R3,000

WINELANDS

Oude Werf RR

South Africa's oldest inn is on oak-lined Church Street in the historic heart of Stellenbosch. It was originally named Ouwe Werf and was established in 1802. It retains a gracious old-world atmosphere, enhanced by period furnishings. Run by the same family for decades, the hotel has just 38 rooms and a welcoming atmosphere. The courtyard coffee garden and the Oude Werf Restaurant serve traditional Cape cuisine at reasonable prices.
✛ 230 C3
✉ 30 Church Street, Stellenbosch
☎ 021 887 4608 ⊕ www.oudewerfhotel.co.za

Oude Werf is South Africa's oldest inn

WHALE COAST

The Marine RRR

This luxury hotel is in an outstanding position overlooking Walker Bay. Furnishings are lavish, with marble bathrooms and chandeliers. Facilities include a spacious garden with a heated pool, two restaurants and a spa. In front is Hermanus's tidal pool where you can swim just 100m (330ft) from a whale, if you're lucky.
✛ 231 D2 ✉ Marine Drive, Hermanus
☎ 028 313 1000
⊕ www.themarinehotel.co.za

GARDEN ROUTE

African Ocean Manor RR–RRR

This stylish guest house on the beachfront offers its guests a fantastic view of the ocean. There are only five rooms and suites, the facilities include a swimming pool and a *braai* area and the breakfast is excellent.
✛ 223 D1 ✉ Bouwer Crescent, Mossel Bay
☎ 044 695 1846 ⊕ www.africanoceans.co.za

Moontide Guest Lodge R

This is an intimate guest house on the edge of Wilderness National Park. The eight rooms and thatched cottages are lovingly decorated with African art. If you fancy something different, you can sleep in a converted boathouse or a unique tree house.
✛ 223 D2 ✉ Southside Lane, Wilderness
☎ 044 877 0361 ⊕ www.moontide.co.za

Peace of Eden Nature Lodge R

Located 9km (6mi) outside of Knysna this eco-vegan forest retreat offers a range of accommodation from rustic chalets to camp tents. Ideal for guests looking for peace in nature.
✛ 223 D1 ✉ 7km (4mi) west of Knysna
☎ 074 755 5859 ⊕ www.peaceofeden.co.za

The Point Hotel R

The Point Hotel has a prime position perched on the rocks with an unbeatable view of the ocean, and you may spot whales in season. There are 48 comfortable rooms and some excellent restaurants nearby.
✛ 223 D1 ✉ Point Road, Mossel Bay
☎ 044 691 3512 ⊕ www.pointhotel.co.za

PORT ELIZABETH

Hacklewood Hill Country House RRR

In a Victorian manor in the suburb of Walmer, Hacklewood Hill is decorated with antiques and paintings, and has beautiful English-style gardens. It is a romantic, intimate place to stay, with just eight immaculate rooms. There's a fine cordon bleu restaurant with an impressive collection of vintage wines.
✛ 223 F2
✉ 152 Prospect Road, Port Elizabeth
☎ 041 581 1300 ⊕ www.hacklewood.co.za

WILD COAST

Buccaneers Backpackers R
Overlooking the beach, this rural backpacker hostel has a rustic feel with wooden-decked bar and a restaurant surrounded by a forest full of birds. There are cosy dorms, doubles, self-catering cottages, or you can camp on platforms beneath the trees. The hostel can organize tours throughout the Wild Coast and sports equipment is available for rental.
🕂 224 C2 ✉ Cintsa ☎ 043 734 3012
🌐 www.cintsa.com

Where to...Eat and Drink

Expect to pay for a two-course meal per person excluding drinks:

R	under R200
RR	R200–R350
RRR	over R350

WINELANDS

Eight Restaurant RRR
This restaurant on the Spier wine estate is housed in a renovated farm barn. The small menu offers dishes (mainly free-range beef) made with seasonal ingredients sourced from the farm. Staff are well trained, friendly and helpful. Guests can also enjoy a pre-booked picnic basket from the restaurant's deli.
🕂 230 B3 ✉ Spier Estate, R310 southwest of Stellenbosch ☎ 021 809 1188
🌐 www.spier.co.za/food/eight-restaurant
🕐 Lunch: Tue–Sun noon–3:30; dinner: Fri–Sun 6:30–9:30, closed Mon

Reuben's RRR
Food lovers from Cape Town make the 45-minute trip to Franschhoek for lunch here at the weekends. Log fires warm the building in winter, while tables spill onto the street in summer. Dishes are refreshingly simple and simply delicious.
🕂 230 C3
✉ 19 Huguenot Street, Franschhoek
☎ 021 876 2393
🌐 www.reubens.co.za
🕐 Daily noon–3, 6:30–9

WHALE COAST

Bientang's Cave RR
Down a steep staircase from Hermanus' cliff top, this restaurant is partially concealed in a cave and the stone platform is on the ocean's edge; it is the perfect vantage point for whale-watching in season.
🕂 231 D2
✉ Below Marine Drive, Hermanus
☎ 028 312 3454 🌐 www.bientangscave.com
🕐 Daily 11–4, and Fri, Sat evenings (weather permitting); reservations recommended

Mogg's Country Cookhouse RR
Just a short drive from Hermanus, this family restaurant serves a hearty but imaginative selection of country food. Reservations are advised.
🕂 231 D2
✉ Hemel-en-Aarde Road, Hermanus
☎ 076 314 0671
🌐 www.moggscookhouse.com
🕐 Daily noon–2:30, dinner by arrangement only

GARDEN ROUTE

34° South RR
This is a very casual, laid-back spot with a wooden deck overlooking Knysna Lagoon. You make up a meal from the treats in the packed fridges in the deli or choose from the menu. Look for specials such as seafood paella, Cajun ostrich or seared tuna.
🕂 223 D1 ✉ Knysna Quays, Knysna
☎ 044 382 7331 🌐 www.34south.biz
🕐 Daily 9am–10pm

Café Gannet RRR
The Protea Hotel's modern Café Gannet is an excellent seafood restaurant with a terrace that has a lovely view over the bay and the Outeniqua mountain range. It is right next to the Bartolomeu Dias Museum, and the staff is welcoming and friendly. Ask for the catch of the day or try their famous seafood casserole. The menu also features oysters, sushi and a few meat dishes.
🕂 223 D1 ✉ Old Post Tree Square, Mossel Bay
☎ 044 691 3738 🌐 www.oldposttree.co.za
🕐 Daily noon–3, 7–10

PORT ELIZABETH & AROUND

Die Walskipper RR
With a simple corrugated-iron roof, shade cloth, and enamel tin plates and cups, this casual restaurant on the beach is a great place to kick your shoes off in the sand and enjoy the ocean views. The simple, tasty food includes sensibly priced seafood and meat.

✛ 223 F1 ✉ Marina Martinique, Jeffrey's Bay ☎ 042 292 0005
🌐 www.walskipper.co.za
🕐 Tue–Sat noon–8, Sun until 3

EAST LONDON

Grazia RR
Its elevated position overlooking the Esplanade means that the tables on the terrace fill up quickly in the evening. Excellent Italian cuisine, from game to seafood, with an eclectic mix of other influences.

✛ 224 C2 ✉ Upper Esplanade
☎ 043 722 2009
🌐 www.graziafinefood.co.za
🕐 Daily 11:30–3, 6:30–10:30

Where to...Shop

WINELANDS

The most interesting shop in Stellenbosch is Oom Samie se Winkel or Uncle Samie's Shop (84 Dorp Street; tel: 021 887 0797), an old-fashioned general store, barely altered since it opened 150 years ago.

Most of Stellenbosch's other shops are centrally situated between Merriman Avenue, Bird and Dorp streets and only 15 minutes away is the region's largest shopping centre, Somerset Mall (tel: 021 852 7114/5; www.somerset-mall.co.za) on the N2 in Somerset West.

A must-stop is the gorgeous Eight to Go Deli on the Spier wine estate south of Stellenbosch, which is full to the brim of African products, often locally made.

In Franschhoek visit Huguenot Fine Chocolates (62 Huguenot Street; tel: 021 876 4096; www.huguenotchocolates. com). The shop produces a delicious range of handcrafted chocolates.

The village centre boasts an array of art shops and galleries, including the Ebony Curated (4 Bordeaux Street; http://ebony curated.com), which showcases local and international artists.

Also worth a visit is Franschhoek Live Craft Centre (Huguenot Road; tel: 021 876 4092), where you watch the resident potter and other craftsmen produce their items and also buy their handicraft.

For serious wine enthusiasts there is La Cotte Inn (Main Road; tel: 021 876 3775; www.lacotte.co.za), with a mind-boggling collection of Cape wines complemented by a vast array of local and imported cheeses.

Meander down Main Street in Paarl where there are soft furnishing, antiques and gift shops.

WHALE COAST

Hermanus has an interesting variety of shops and art galleries and the Fisherman's Village Craft Market (8:30–3) is held every weekend at Lemm's Corner. Enjoy the market hustle and bustle as you browse the crafts, curios and antiques, you'll be sure to find the per-fect souvenir.

The Village Square (www.village-square. co.za) shopping mall has boutiques, gift shops and restaurants.

GARDEN ROUTE

The towns along the Garden Route have a wide selection of shops selling anything from beachwear to African trinkets.

The Garden Route Mall (tel: 044 887 0044; www.gardenroutemall.co.za) is the biggest in the region, and is located on the N2 at the turn-off to George. It has in excess of 125 shops and restaurants.

Knysna is well known for its artists and craftsmen and there are galleries throughout the town and many shops

Ceramics in a décor and souvenir shop

around the waterfront development; roadside stalls sell carved wooden figures and drums.

The Knysna African Arts & Craft Market is on the corner of George Rex Street and Vigilance Drive.

Knysna is also famous for its furniture made from indigenous timber, and Timber Village (tel: 044 382 5649; www.timber village.co.za), in the Welbedacht Valley 3km (2mi) from Knysna, is home to a community of wood craftsmen.

In Plettenberg Bay, the main mall is Market Square, and be sure to visit the Old Nick Village on the N2 (tel: 044 533 1395; www.oldnickvillage.co.za) for the galleries, studios, a weaving museum and a restaurant in lush gardens.

PORT ELIZABETH & AROUND

Jeffrey's Bay, as South Africa's surfing capital, has factory outlets for the inter-national surf brands Billabong (2a Da Gama Road; tel: 042 200 2600) and Quiksilver (10 St Croix Street; tel: 042 293 4116; www. quiksilver.co.za/stores).

Port Elizabeth is a large city and has several giant shopping malls with the Boardwalk Casino and Entertainment World (www.suninternational.com) on the beachfront in Summerstrand being one of the most popular.

WILD COAST

Hemingways Mall (www.hemingwaysmall. co.za) in East London has over 200 stores.

Where to...Go Out

MUSIC, THEATRE & FESTIVALS

Stellenbosch's AmaZink Township Theatre (http://amazinklive.co.za) offers an authentic township theatre experience while the Stellenbosch International Chamber Music Festival (tel: 072 531 3235; www.sicmf.co.za) in September concentrates on art exhibitions and chamber music. In Hermanus, the Whale Festival (tel: 071 606 3261; http://hermanus whalefestival.co.za) in September draws theatre, and musical and dancing groups, many of which perform on the street. The Barns Venue in Mossel Bay (tel: 044 698 1022; www.reedvalley.co.za) is in an actual barnyard on a farm 3km (2mi) from town. See cabaret, theatre and music in Knysna during July's 10-day Oyster Festival (www.oysterfestival. co.za) and at the 5-day gay Pink Loerie Mardi Gras (www.pinkloerie.co.za), held end April/ early May. There are several live performance venues in Port Elizabeth and festivals include a Shakespearean Festival (tel: 041 364 3900; www.facebook.com/PEShakespeare) in February and the four-day Nelson Mandela Bay Splash Festival (tel: 041 393 4844; www. splashfestival.com) over the Easter weekend. South Africa's not-to-be-missed festival is the 10-day National Arts Festival (www.national artsfestival.co.za) in Grahamstown (June/July).

NIGHTLIFE

Nightlife is limited in the rural areas but the towns have a few nightspots.

In Stellenbosch, Aandklas (43 Bird Street; tel: 021 883 3545; www.facebook.com/ aandklasstb) gets packed with students who come for the grungy bands and cheap beer on tap. Mossel Bay is home to the Garden Route Casino (www.tsogosun.com), and Knysna has more than 50 pubs and restau-rants including the popular Project Bar Lounge (Thesen Island; tel: 44 302 5814; www.theprojectbar.co.za). Port Elizabeth's nightlife is based in the Boardwalk Casino and Entertainment World (tel: 041 507 7777; www.suninternational.com; daily 24 hours).

The Drakensberg traverses over 1,000km (620mi) inland from the South African Highlands down to the eastern coast

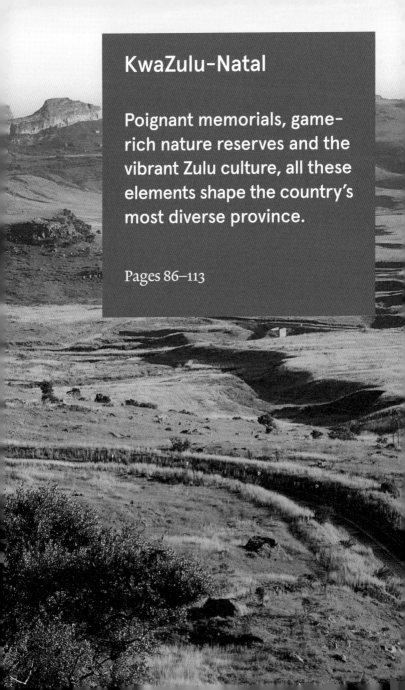

KwaZulu-Natal

Poignant memorials, game-rich nature reserves and the vibrant Zulu culture, all these elements shape the country's most diverse province.

Pages 86–113

Getting Your Bearings

KwaZulu-Natal has a lot to offer: a tropical climate, long sandy beaches, pristine wilderness areas and more game reserves than any other province in South Africa. The area's abundant natural water supply also contributed to its development, with 21 per cent of the population living here – the majority being Zulu. The original Zulu Kingdom was extended and consolidated with the creation of the province. The Durban metropolitan area is also the centre of South Africa's Indian population.

The largest (almost 11.5 million) ethnic group in South Africa is the Zulu, and in the early 19th century, King Shaka led them in violent warfare, conquering and controlling large parts of southern Africa. The Zulu's oldest political rivals are the Xhosa. In 1994, animosities between the two groups went so far that their leader, Mangosuthu Buthelezi, risked a civil war to prevent a Xhosa-dominated ANC. It was only after Nelson Mandela succeeded in including Buthelezi in the government, that the unrest came to an end.

Durban and the southern coast are heavily populated with a string of holiday resorts. The north coast, by contrast, is relatively untouched with much of it protected in parks and reserves. The most important of which is the iSimangaliso Wetland Park (formerly the Greater St Lucia Wetland Park), today a UNESCO World Heritage Site listed for its exceptional biodiversity.

Inland the N3 highway heads north from Durban to Johannesburg through the pretty farmlands of the Natal Midlands, which have the charm of a bygone era. To the southwest and encircling Lesotho, the mountains in the uKhahlamba-Drakensberg Park soar to over 3,000m (9,800ft). To the northeast the now peaceful rolling green pastures and historic towns of the Battlefields region testify to the bloody 19th-century wars between the Zulus, the British and the Boers. The Boers (*boere* is Afrikaans for farmer) are the descendants of the 17th-century Dutch settlers of the Cape. This group still represent an important part of South Africa's white minority, and retain their customs, language (Afrikaans) and the traditions of the Dutch Reformed Church.

My Day
with Hippos, Eagles and Whales

The biodiversity of the iSimangaliso Wetland Park is exceptional and you are almost guaranteed to photograph all of the Big Seven. That means you'll see the Big Five – lion, leopard, buffalo, rhino and elephant – plus the great white shark and the southern right whale. The charming Lodge Afrique (www.lodgeafrique.com) in the small town of St Lucia is the ideal base to use when exploring the park.

7am: The Adventure Begins

Set out as early as possible after breakfast – the earlier you leave, the more game you'll encounter. Your hosts will provide you with a lavish packed lunch, so grab your bathing suit, and drive north along the main road. At about 2km (1.25mi) outside of St Lucia you'll reach Bhangazi Gate, the park's entrance, where you'll need to pay an entrance fee (R48/person, R58/vehicle).

8am: The Journey is the Destination

Drive slowly (maximum speed is 40km/h (25mph) on the gravel roads, 50km/h (30mph) on tarred) and pay close attention to the landscape. After a short time, your eyes will become accustomed to the

11am: Picnic Between
Sand Dunes

Lake St Lucia

iSimangaliso

10 km
5 mi

Wetland Park

Bhangazi

11am

Cape Vidal

Mfazana Hide
10:30am

10:30am: Very Close Encounters

Amazibu Pan

St Lucia
R618

Bhangazi Gate

8am: The Journey is the
Destination

iSimangaliso

Wetland Park

8am

St Lucia Tours &
Charters

Braza

Start

ST LUCIA

Lodge Afrique
7am

End

7am: The Adventure Begins

500 m
500 yd

Take a stroll along the beach before you have your picnic between the dunes

scenery and you will start to recognise unusual patterns and movements. Could that be a buffalo? You may spot impala nervously sniffing the air before darting across the road or a waterbuck cautiously drinking at a watering hole. Follow the signs for the various loop roads that lead off the main road, such as the one to the Amazibu Pan, a shallow lake where hippos often take a dip and where you may spy wildebeest and zebras among the tall grass.

10:30am: Very Close Encounters

Shortly before Cape Vidal you will reach the Mfazana Hide, where there is always a good chance of seeing rhino. The observation hide is a deck covered in wood strips with viewing slits so that visitors are camouflaged as they watch the comings and goings of the pan's game. The marshy pan also attracts other game, such as warthogs and kudu, as well as a great variety of colourful birds. With a little bit of luck, you may see a rhino standing right in front of your observation slit, or perhaps even a lion!

11am: Picnic Between Sand Dunes

Next up is a swim at Cape Vidal, where there are some sand dunes as high as 150m (490ft). It may look idyllic, but beware of the strong currents, and remember that out beyond the surf there are also great white sharks. After your swim, you can enjoy your picnic and while you snack, fish eagles may be circling

Centre above: A boat trip to see crocodiles and hippos
Centre below: Hippo mother and calf. Right: The mighty fluke of a diving whale

above you, guinea fowl may venture close, as will the baboons that like to make off with any of the leftovers. At around 1pm, head back to St Lucia, along the way you will probably encounter more of Africa's wildlife, maybe even elephants.

2pm: Whales or Hippos?
Your afternoon activities will depend on the time of year. Between June and November you can head out to the best whale-watching spots with St Lucia Tours & Charters (advantagetours.co.za/st-lucia/whale-watching; 2–3 hours; R1,150). If the majestic marine mammals have already moved on, you can opt for a boat trip to see hippos and crocodiles (advantagetours.activitar.com; 2 hours; R440). Afternoon tea and snacks are usually provided on these excursions.

5pm: Hunger Pangs
In the countryside, South Africans head to bed after an early dinner, so with this in mind you should take an early stroll through St Lucia before sitting down down to dinner at around 6:30pm. If you fancy a tasty Portuguese or African dish from neighbouring Mozambique then head over to Braza (73 McKenzie Street; tel: 035 590 1242).

❹ ★★ uKhahlamba–Drakensberg Park

Don't Miss	Awe-inspiring mountainous landscapes
Why	Ancient geology, bizarrely eroded rock formations
Time	Two days
When	In the South African spring or autumn
What Else	San rock art
Souvenir	Views of South Africa's highest peaks and mountains

The Drakensberg traverses over 1,000km (620mi) inland from the South African Highlands down to the eastern coast. Its northern part, the Mpumalanga Drakensberg, includes the Blyde River Canyon Nature Reserve while the southern part, the Natal Drakensberg, has dramatic craggy mountains that soar over 3,000m (10,000ft) and some spectacular waterfalls. The area was proclaimed a UNESCO World Heritage Site in 2000 for its natural beauty.

Rural village life in the Drakensberg, about 40km/25mi west of Winterton

The name, meaning "dragon mountains" in Afrikaans, was coined when an early farmer reported seeing a dragon flying above the misty peaks. The area is divided into three sections: the Northern Berg with the Royal Natal National Park, the

Central Berg (Champagne Castle, Cathedral Peak, Giants Castle) and the Southern Berg (Loteni Nature Reserve, Kamberg Nature Reserve, Mzimkulwana Nature Reserve). The uKhahlamba-Drakensberg Park encompasses 12 nature reserves. The Zulu name *uKhahlamba* means "fortress wall of spears", an appropriate description of the towering mountains and their near vertical cliffs and buttresses. Each park has its own scenic attractions and accommodation in the way of a camp managed by KZN Wildlife, but you can also opt to stay over in the more exclusive country hotels nearby. Access depends on which direction you're coming from, but most people approach from the N3 highway that links Johannesburg and Durban from where there are many roads heading west into the mountains.

The Devil's Tooth rock formation, part of the Amphitheatre, in the Northern Berg

Rock Amphitheatre

One of the best parks in the Northern Berg is the Royal Natal National Park, which is dominated by the view to the famous Amphitheatre; a 5km (3mi) sheer cliff rising 1,000m (3,280ft) between two brooding mountains. The impressive Tugela Falls, the world's second highest waterfall, plunges 947m (3,110ft) down the rock wall and there's a spectacularly beautiful hike to the top of the Amphitheatre, which starts at the Mahai Camp parking area. It takes about five hours to do the return trip, and the trail, which includes a scramble up two chain ladders, takes you to the top of the Tugela Falls. This is by far the easiest day hike to the top of the Drakensberg escarpment.

Mythological San Symbols

South of Royal Natal in the Central Berg, Mlambonja Wilderness Area is accessed from Winterton. The peaks offer challenging hikes and this is one of the best places to learn about the San rock paintings in the uKhahlamba-Drakensberg Park. The Didima San Rock Art Centre at Didima Camp is in a reconstructed cave and showcases reproductions of some of the paintings, there are also audio-visual presentations. The San, also known as the Bushmen, roamed the uKhahlamba-Drakensberg Mountains for thousands of years before the Boer and Zulu arrived in the 19th century. Today there remains a fascinating legacy of their culture in their magnificent rock art (paintings, engravings and carvings) found in caves and under rocky overhangs, many dating back 4,000 years. There are over 35,000 documented rock paintings scattered around the park.

A crystal-clear waterfall in the wooded foothills of the Drakensberg Mountains

Further south, the road to the Mdedelelo Wilderness Area and Monk's Cowl is dotted with luxury resorts and is dubbed Champagne Valley. It's where the Central Drakensberg Information Centre is located, and is home to the Drakensberg Boys' Choir boarding school.

Nottingham Road is the access town to the Mkhomazi Wilderness Area where the tallest mountain in southern Africa, Thabana-Ntlenyana (3,482m/11,420ft), is clearly visible. Trout fishing is popular in the foothills of the Kamberg Nature Reserve where there is another San Rock Art Centre from where you can take a guided walk to see some paintings.

Sani Pass Adventure

Underberg and Himeville, with a fine rural museum, are the gateway to the Southern Berg region. Here the rugged Sani Pass winds up an increasingly narrow V-shaped valley flanked by towering buttresses. You can go on an organized four-wheel drive day excursion (tel: 033 701 1064; www.sanipass-tours.co.za) over into Lesotho. At the top is a village where you can meet the friendly Basotho people.

INSIDER TIP Enjoy tea and take in the views from the **Sani Mountain Lodge** (tel: 073 541 8620; www.sanimountain.co.za; R–RR) at the top of Sani Pass.

San rock art often depicts animals and human figures

✚ 225 D4

KZN Wildlife
☎ 033 845 1000 ⊕ www.kznwildlife.com

Didima San Rock Art Centre
✉ Didima Camp
☎ 036 488 8025
⊕ www.didima.info
🕐 Daily 8–4 🎫 R60

Central Drakensberg Information Centre
✉ Thokozisa Centre,
R600 ☎ 036 488 1207
⊕ www.cdic.co.za
🕐 Daily 9–5

Drakensberg Boys' Choir
✉ R600 ☎ 036 468 1012
⊕ http://dbchoir.com
🕐 Concerts: 3:30 Wed during term time
🎫 R120

Himeville Museum
✉ Arbuckle Street
☎ 033 702 1184
🕐 Tue–Sat 9–3, Sun 9–12:30 🎫 Free

Kamberg San Rock Art Centre
✉ Kamberg Nature Reserve
☎ 033 267 7251
🕐 Daily tours 8:30, 11 and 1:30
🎫 Park entrance R80

Himeville Museum
✉ Arbuckle Street, Himeville
☎ 033 702 1184
🕐 Tue–Sat 9–3, Sun 9–12:30
🎫 Free

❼ ★★ Zululand & Maputaland

Don't Miss	Engaging with South Africa's largest ethnic group
Why	Traditional villages and a subtropical national park
Time	Two to five days
When	In the drier months from May to September
What Else	Coral reef diving
Souvenir	Vibrant handcrafted bead jewellery

The holiday resorts on the north KwaZulu-Natal coast taper out to wetlands, lagoons, forests and isolated beaches where turtles, dolphins, sharks and even crocodiles frolic. This is also the traditional stronghold of the Zulu people.

Eshowe, about 150km (95mi) north of Durban, is the gateway to Zululand. About 15km (9mi) further north of Eshowe is Shakaland, a popular Zulu theme park, named after King Shaka, founder of the 19th-century empire for which the region is named. Further north, the Hluhluwe-iMfolozi National Park, the oldest nature reserve in South African (established in 1895), was instrumental in saving the white rhino from extinction.

Close encounter with a crocodile hatchling in the iSimangaliso Wetland Park

The iSimangaliso Wetland Park, a UNESCO World Heritage Site, protects a mosaic of forest, savannah, dune, mangrove, freshwater and marine habitats centred on a series of coastal wetlands running north from the St Lucia Estuary. Set at the estuary mouth, St Lucia village is a useful springboard for hiking or exploring by boat. For more reliable game viewing, Mkhuze Game Reserve harbours rhino and elephant.

The remote north of the iSimangaliso Wetland Park is known as Maputaland. The best-known site here is Sodwana Bay with Africa's southernmost coral reefs.

The First Light

As day breaks in the Hluhluwe-Imfolozi
Park, and your open vehicle bumps over the
steep terrain, the first rays of the morning
sun make the dew drops on the high grass
shimmer like cut diamonds. The crisp air is
cut through by the screech of a bird on a
branch, a warthog family trots calmly along
the road…then the vehicle stops and, in a
nearby clearing, you see a few white rhinos
grazing on some foliage. An extraordinary
and unforgettable experience.

Anglers waiting
for a bite in
St Lucia

West of Kosi Bay, the <u>Lubombo Transfrontier
Conservation Area</u> is a cross-border reserve linking
South Africa's Ndumo Game Reserve and Tembe Elephant
Park to Mozambique's Maputo Special Reserve via the
Futi Corridor.

INSIDER TIP The restaurant in St Lucia's **Elephant Lake Hotel**
(tel: 035 590 1001; www.elephantlakestlucia.co.za; RR) is a
great spot.

✚ 229 E1 (Zululand)
✚ 229 E2 (Maputaland)
❶ Information for all parks:
www.kznwildlife.com ❶ Oct–Mar daily
5am–7pm; Apr–Sep 6–6

Shakaland
✚ 229 E1 (Eshowe) ✉ R66 near Eshowe
☎ 035 460 0912 ⊕ www.aha.co.za/
shakaland ❶ Tours 11–2 and noon–3
✦ R560, lunch included

Hluhluwe-iMfolozi National Park
✚ 229 E/F2
✉ 280km (174mi) north of Durban
☎ 035 562 0848 ⊕ www.kznwildlife.com
❶ Nov–Feb daily 5am–7pm;
Mar–Oct 6–6 ✦ R210

iSimangaliso Wetland Park
✚ 229 F2
✉ 245km (152mi) north of Durban

☎ 035 590 1633
⊕ http://isimangaliso.com
❶ Times vary at different locations
within the park
✦ Depends on the park section
R27–R48 (some sections are free)

Mkhuze Game Reserve
✚ 229 F2
✉ 335km (208mi) north of Durban
☎ 033 845 1000 ⊕ www.kznwildlife.com
❶ Oct–Mar daily 5am–7pm;
Apr–Sep 6–6 ✦ R45

**Lubombo Transfrontier
Conservation Area**
✚ 229 F2 ✉ Turn off the N2 at Jozini
and follow road signs ☎ 035 572 1560
⊕ www.peaceparks.org
❶ Tembe: Oct–Mar daily 5am–7pm;
Apr–Sep 6–6. Ndumo: 8–noon, 1–4
✦ Tembe: R50; Ndumo: R60

❿ ★★ Durban

Don't Miss	An exuberant, multicultural melting pot
Why	The Indian market, British architecture, Zulu rickshaws and great beaches
Time	One to three days
When	In the drier months from May to September
What Else	A day at the beach
Souvenir	Lots of spices

Durban is South Africa's third largest city; a modern, vibrant and colourful metropolis with an unmistakeably African and Asian feel to it. It boasts a subtropical climate, stylish cafés, chic restaurants and some good shopping opportunities – and wide golden beaches along the warm Indian Ocean.

In December 1497 Vasco da Gama sailed along the coast and, as he saw the bay on Christmas Day, he named it Port Natal.

It was not until 1823, when a few British traders set up a settlement, that the area developed into a port and trading centre for ivory. In 1835 the British renamed the settlement Durban in honour of Sir Benjamin D'Urban, governor of the Cape

Durban is known as Surf City

Colony. Durban grew quickly in the 1860s when the British brought in thousands of Indian indentured labourers to work the region's sugar plantations. Today part of the greater eThekweni municipality, Durban has the largest Indian community in Africa, and original shopping arcades of Indian traders thrive around Victoria, Queen and Grey streets. The Juma Masjid Mosque is the largest mosque in the southern hemisphere, and Victoria Street Market sells Indian spices and snacks. The old neo-baroque City Hall is now home to the Natural Science Museum and the Durban Art Gallery, with a fine collection of European-style paintings and a wide range of African art.

West of the centre is KwaMuhle Museum in what was the notorious Department of Native Affairs during apartheid; exhibits show the oppressive administration of the black population of Durban during the 20th century. On the port side of the city on Victoria Embankment is the Victorian Da Gama Clock, erected to commemorate the 400th anniversary of the Portuguese seafarer sighting the bay. Further down the embankment is the shopping mall at Wilson's Wharf and the Yacht Mole where you can watch the comings and goings of a huge variety of craft, see the harbour at work and buy fresh fish from the fish shop.

The Golden Mile extends along Marine Parade (between Snell Parade and Erskine Parade) and the beachfront is lined with hotels, high-rise apartments, restaurants and bars. Look out for the rickshaw pullers with their giant hats and vibrant costumes: you can bargain with them for a short ride (about R50 per person for a 5-minute ride; photographs cost extra). The beach is wide and sandy and there are demarcated areas

The ornate 19th-century Da Gama Clock on Victoria Embankment

for swimming, sunbathing and surfing, and it's punctuated with a number of piers that are popular with anglers. The paved promenade has various attractions strung along it, from waterslides and saltwater paddling pools to snake parks and fairground rides.

The uShaka Marine World has aquariums, a reptile exhibit, a dolphinarium and seal tank, and on Battery Beach, the Suncoast Casino and Entertainment World has restaurants, a multi-screen cinema, a boardwalk and Waterworld with a variety of slides.

On the Umgeni River in Durban North, the Umgeni River Bird Park has a spectacular collection of more than 800 exotic and indigenous birds to view from a network of paths. The highlight is the free-flight show when the larger raptors, cranes, storks and owls hop onto a stage and fly over the audience.

In Berea the Durban Botanic Gardens have subtropical plants, orchids and a collection of cycads. There is a fine tearoom, pleasant picnic spots and the Japanese Gardens have an enchanting atmosphere with ponds and oriental designs.

Further north, Umhlanga Rocks has a couple of worthwhile diversions. Lose yourself for a few hours in Gateway, the largest shopping mall in the southern hemisphere. Alternatively, visit the KwaZulu-Natal Sharks Board, a one-of-its-kind institution that looks after more than 400 shark nets along 50 beaches on the KwaZulu-Natal coast. You can visit the information centre to learn about

The Royal Natal Yacht Club affords beautiful views of Durban's modern urban skyline at night

sharks and arrange to go out on a boat with the staff to service the nets.

Resorts, holiday apartments and caravan parks follow the beaches south from Durban. The Aliwal Shoal and the wreck of the steamer Nebo that sank in 1884 lie 5km (3mi) off the coast of Umkomaas and are popular with scuba divers; ragged tooth sharks are often spotted. Further south the ribbon of development continues between Scottburgh and Port Edward, broken by banana and eucalyptus plantations. On offer here is diving, surfing or jet-skiing in the ocean and endless hours on the sandy beaches. Margate, one of the more upmarket resorts, is a popular holiday. Port Edward with its palm-fringed beach marks the border with the Wild Coast in the Eastern Cape Province.

 INSIDER TIP ▶ Relax at the **BAT (Bartle Arts Trust) Centre** on Victoria Embankment for the fine harbour views, live music and craft shops (tel: 031 332 0451; www.batcentre.co.za; R).

ℹ ✚ 229 E3

Tourist Junction
✉ 90 Florida Rd ☎ 031 322 6164
⊕ www.durbanexperience.co.za
🕐 Mon–Fri 8–4:30, Sat, Sun 9–1

Natural Science Museum
✉ City Hall, 234 Anton Lembede St
☎ 031 311 2256 🕐 Daily 9–4 ✦ Free

Durban Art Gallery
✉ City Hall, 234 Anton Lembede St
☎ 031 311 2264
🕐 Mon–Sat 8:30–4, Sun 11–4 ✦ Free

KwaMuhle Museum
✉ 130 Bram Fischer Rd ☎ 031 311 2237
⊕ http://durbanhistorymuseums.org.za
🕐 Mon–Fri 8:30–4, Sat 8.30–12:30
✦ Free

uShaka Marine World
✉ Beachfront ☎ 031 328 8000

⊕ www.ushakamarineworld.co.za
🕐 9–5 ✦ R209

Suncoast Casino and Entertainment World
✉ Marine Parade ☎ 031 328 3000
⊕ www.tsogosun.com

Umgeni River Bird Park
✉ 490 Riverside Rd, Durban North
☎ 031 579 4600 ⊕ www.umgeniriver
birdpark.co.za 🕐 9–5, free-flight bird
show 11 and 2 ✦ R58

Durban Botanic Gardens
✉ 9A John Zikhali Rd, Berea
☎ 031 322 4021
⊕ https://durbanbotanicgardens.org.za
🕐 Daily 7:30–5:15 ✦ Free

KwaZulu-Natal Sharks Board
✉ Herrwood Drive
☎ 031 566 0400 ⊕ www.shark.co.za
🕐 Mon–Fri 8–4 ✦ R45

㉙ Battlefields

Don't Miss	An understanding of South Africa's settler history
Why	Museums and memorial sites that commemorate battles
Time	One day
When	Arrive early as most of the museums close at 4pm
What Else	Tranquil landscape of rolling fields and pastures
In Short	Emotional and thought provoking

The rolling hills of the Midlands witnessed some of the country's bloodiest battles during the Zulu-Boer War, the Anglo-Zulu War and the Anglo-Boer War.

The violent military clashes continued for over 70 years and there are more than 50 battlefield sites. There are 14 historic towns, including Ladysmith and Dundee, and some informative museums. The area is best explored by self-driving. The Blood River Monument consists of Voortrekker wagons arranged as they were on the day of the famous battle. On the opposite side of the river, the Ncome Museum explores the conflict from a Zulu perspective. The British were badly defeated at Isandlwana in 1879 during the Anglo-Zulu War. At Rorke's Drift a tiny museum displays pictures of the battle and war memorabilia. The Talana Hill Museum is set in an 8ha (20-acre) park and has 17 buildings. The Siege Museum in Ladysmith has a varied collection of war memorabilia.

INSIDER TIP Sit down for a tasty lunch or a cup of tea in the **Miners' Rest** restaurant, housed in a 1914 corrugated iron miner's home at the Talana Hill Museum.

Ncome Museum
✛ 229 E1 ✉ 48km (30mi) from Dundee toward Vryheid ☎ 034 271 8121 ⊕ www.ncomemuseum.co.za ◷ Daily 8–4 ✦ Free

Isandlwana
✛ 229 E1 ✉ 80km (50mi) southeast of Dundee

☎ 034 271 8165 ◷ Daily 8–4 ✦ R35

Rorke's Drift Museum
✛ 229 E1 ✉ 42km (26mi) southeast from Dundee ☎ 034 642 1687 ◷ Daily 8–4 ✦ R35

Talana Hill Museum
✛ 229 D2 ✉ R33, Dundee

☎ 034 212 2654 ⊕ www.talana.co.za ◷ Mon–Fri 8–4:30, Sat, Sun 9–noon ✦ R35

Siege Museum
✛ 229 D1 ✉ Murchison Street, Ladysmith ☎ 036 637 2992 ◷ Mon–Fri 9–4, Sat 9–1 ✦ R11

At Your Leisure

30 Oribi Gorge Nature Reserve

Formed by the Umzimkulwana River, the 400m-deep (1,312ft) Oribi Gorge has magnificent red-orange sandstone cliffs, which tower over a valley lined with trees, flowers and ferns. Several waterfalls gush into the river, which has rapids, pools and sandbanks. There are some well-marked hiking and mountain bike trails, picnic spots, horseback rides and white-water rafting options. If you are adventure-minded, you can try the 120m (400ft) zip line, go abseiling, or try the gorge swing that takes you on a 100m (330ft) arc into the gorge and past Lehr's Falls.

✠ 225 D3
✉ Off the N2, 21km (13mi) from Port Shepstone ☎ 072 042 9390
⊕ www.kznwildlife.com ⏲ Oct–Mar 5am–7pm; April–Sep 6–6 🍴 R60
**Wild 5 Adventures
(Wild Swing/Bungee)**
☎ 082 566 74 24
⊕ www.wild5adventures.co.za
🍴 Abseiling R500; swing: R650

---

31 Valley of 1,000 Hills

The Valley of 1,000 Hills is a region along the R103 about 35km (22mi) from the northern outskirts of Durban where hundreds of low hills spill down to the Umgeni River and its tributaries. The highlights here are the undulating hillsides dotted with settlements and the opportunity to learn about Zulu culture. You can follow signs for the 1,000 Hills Experience to enjoy the views and stop at the many gift shops and tea gardens. At the PheZulu Safari Park is a reconstruction of a Zulu village with beehive huts; a guide explains Zulu beliefs and rituals before a show of dancing. There's also an animal and reptile park, restaurant and curio shop.

A three-hour ride through the picturesque landscape with Umgeni Steam Railway is an impressive experience. On the last Sunday of each month trains depart from Kloof Station to Inchanga return (morning and afternoons; tel: 082 353 6003; www.umgenisteam railway.com; R240; children R170).

✠ 225 E4
PheZulu Safari Park
✉ 5 Old Main Road, Botha's Hill
☎ 031 777 1000
⊕ www.phezulusafaripark.co.za
⏲ 8–4:30; shows at 10, 11:30, 2 and 3:30
🍴 Zulu Village and dance shows: R130, combined ticket with reptile park: R150; game drive R240

The undulating landscape of the Valley of 1,000 Hills

32 Pietermaritzburg

With its beautiful Victorian brick buildings and tree-lined streets, Pietermaritzburg – once the administrative capital of the Colony of Natal – today still retains an old-fashioned British feel, were it not for its lively African street life. But with its large, vibrant Indian community, Asia also seems to be close at hand. Of interest are the Parliament Buildings built in 1887 with soaring columns and copper domes, and the City Hall built in 1900 entirely of red bricks and boasting some fine stained-glass windows. On Church Street is a statue of Gandhi, who travelled to South Africa in April 1893. He was forced to leave the train at Pietermaritzburg after he was expelled from the whites only First Class (for which he had a valid ticket). This incident sparked off his idea of passive resistance. The Voortrekker/Msunduzi Museum, set in a 1905 former girls' school, houses an interesting local history section.

The dramatic 95m (312ft) Howick Falls

33 Howick

The small unassuming rural town of Howick, 18km (11mi) north of Pietermaritzburg, is famous for two things – the attractive Howick Falls, and the place just out of town on a quiet country road where Nelson Mandela was arrested in 1962. He was disguised as a driver when he was stopped by police, who were working on a tip-off. Today a monument marks the spot. The Howick Falls dominate the centre of town where the Umgeni River spills dramatically 95m (312ft) into a gorge.

✝ 225 D4
✉ 177 Chief Albert Luthuli Street
☎ 033 345 1348
🌐 www.pmbtourism.co.za
🕐 Mon–Fri 8–5, Sat 8–1
Voortrekker/Msunduzi Museum
✉ 351 Langalibalele Street
☎ 033 345 1348
🌐 www.msunduzimuseum.org.za
🕐 Mon–Fri 9–4, Sat 9–1
🎫 R10

✝ 225 D4
Midlands Meander Association
☎ 033 330 8195
🌐 https://midlandsmeander.co.za

Where to...Stay

Expect to pay in high season per double room per night

R   under R1,500
RR   R1,500–R3,000
RRR   over R3,000

DURBAN

A room in the Concierge Hotel

Concierge Hotel RR
This boutique hotel is a little tucked away from the hustle and bustle. It has twelve contemporary rooms, some with verandas. Its garden courtyard makes it an oasis of peace in the middle of the busy metropolis; the adjoining Freedom Café serves a selection burgers. The quirky hotel's designer credentials – every furniture piece is custom-made – make it one of the coolest places in town.
+ 225 E4
✉ 37–43 St Mary's Ave, Morningside
☎ 031 309 44 53
⊕ www.the-concierge.co.za

Quarters RR
A stylish boutique hotel in Durban's stately Morningside suburb, Quarters is housed in four restored Victorian homes with lattice wrap-around verandas, shady courtyards and gardens full of tropical palms. Each of the 25 rooms has been individually decorated in unfussy modern designs. There's a brasserie that serves tasty, traditional cuisine throughout the day and it's in an excellent location right in the middle of the restaurant district.
+ 225 E4
✉ 101 Florida Road, Morningside
☎ 031 303 5246 ⊕ www.quarters.co.za

ZULULAND & MAPUTALAND

Ghost Mountain Inn R–RR
An informal and affordable 4-star country inn in Mkhuze village, just 20 minutes' drive from the only gate to Mkhuze Game Reserve, Ghost Mountain also makes a good springboard for overnight stays deeper in Maputaland. The smartly decorated rooms are scattered around the garden. There's a pool, a bar, a restaurant and beauty spa.
+ 229 F2
✉ Mkhuze, off the N2 ☎ 035 573 1025
⊕ www.ghostmountaininn.co.za

Hilltop Camp R–RR
This camp is run by Far & Wild Safaris and is in the Hluhluwe-iMfolozi National Park. It has a stunning location with fabulous views over the bush. Accommodation is in simple but comfortable self-catering chalets. Facilities include a central restaurant, bar and pool.
+ 229 F2 ✉ In the northern Hluhluwe section of the park ☎ 031 208 3684
⊕ www.hilltopcamp.co.za

Kosi Forest Lodge RRR
Easily one of the most gorgeous places to stay in KwaZulu-Natal, this lodge is set in the shady sand forest overlooking Lake Shengeza. The 8 luxurious suites, scattered among trees, are under wood and canvas with open-air bathrooms and lit by twinkling lanterns. Activities include canoeing, fishing and snorkelling.
+ 229 F2 ✉ Kosi Bay Nature Reserve
☎ 035 474 1473 ⊕ www.kosiforestlodge.co.za

Makakatana Bay Lodge RRR
Enjoy super luxury at one of the few privately run lodges in the iSimangaliso Wetland Park, set in an idyllic dune forest. The eight spacious suites are linked by elevated boardwalks and come with private wooden decks and outside showers and a writing desk.
✤ 229 F1
✉ Off the Charters Creek road
☎ 035 550 4189
🌐 www.makakatana.com

BATTLEFIELDS

Isandlwana Lodge RR
This double-storey stone and thatch lodge is carved into the rock where the Zulu commander stood when he started the Battle of Isandlwana on the 22nd of January 1879. The lodge's 12 en-suite rooms have balconies and are decorated in a blend of traditional and modern styles. Facilities include a well-appointed pool, restaurant and bar.
✤ 2229 E1
✉ 80km (50mi) southeast of Dundee
☎ 034 271 8301
🌐 www.isandlwana.co.za

MIDLANDS & UKHAHLAMBA-DRAKENSBERG

The Cavern RR
Adjacent to the Royal Natal National Park, these comfortable thatched cottages are scattered through mature gardens with mountain views. Rates represent excellent value as they include three meals a day.
✤ 228 C1 ✉ Off the R74
☎ 036 438 6270 or 083 701 5724
🌐 www.cavern.co.za

Fordoun RRR
Fordoun lies between the central uKhahlamba-Drakensberg and Howick. The luxury rooms are in restored farm buildings. There's an intimate and lovingly decorated restaurant and the spa has all sorts of treats.
✤ 225 D4
✉ Nottingham Road ☎ 033 266 6217
🌐 http://fordoun.com

Where to...Eat and Drink

Expect to pay for a two-course meal per person excluding drinks:
R   under R200
RR   R200–R350
RRR over R350

DURBAN

Green Mango RR–RRR
This small, intimate restaurant in the Avonmore Centre serves excellent Japanese (very good sushi) and Thai cuisine. Try a Thai-styled grilled kebab or a spicy fish curry.
✤ 225 E4
✉ 9th Avenue, Avonmore Centre, Morningside
☎ 031 312 7054
🌐 www.thegreenmango.co.za
🕐 Daily noon–2:30, 6–9:30

Ile Maurice RR–RRR
Positioned to take advantage of the sea views, and featuring island-style décor, this restaurant focuses mainly on freshly caught line fish and seafood dishes. The cuisine is a unique blend of South African and Mauritian dishes. There is also a selection of meat dishes and remember to save room for the tempting desserts. Reservations essential.
✤ 225 E4
✉ 9 McCausland Cresent, Umhlanga Rocks
☎ 031 561 7606
🌐 https://ilemauricerestaurant.co.za
🕐 Tue–Sun 12:15–2:15, 6:30–9:30

Kashmir RR
An elegant restaurant (formal table settings, a rose on each table) with a veranda overlooking the sea. Serving mainly North Indian cuisine – the curries are considered the best Durban – and the bread is freshly baked (order the delicious garlic *naan*). Top-notch quality and excellent presentation.
✤ 225 E4
✉ 11 McCausland Crescent, Umhalanga Rocks

☎ 031 561 7486
⏱ Daily 8:30–11

Mali's Indian Restaurant RR

Durban is famous for its authentic Indian food. At this restaurant in a converted house you'll find a mix of north and south Indian dishes; some say it's the best Indian restaurant in town.

☩ 225 E4
✉ 77 Smiso Nkwanyana Road, Morningside
☎ 031 312 8535
🌐 www.facebook.com/malisindian
⏱ Tue–Sun 12:30–3:30, 5:30–10

Roma Revolving Restaurant RR

The décor is a little dated, but you can't beat the view over Durban Harbour 32 floors below. Delightfully old-fashioned set menus include the likes of prawn cocktail or pâté followed by steak, or pasta and something decadent from the dessert trolley. The à la carte menu offers more adventurous dishes. The restaurant takes an hour to complete its 360-degree circuit.

☩ 225 E4
✉ Victoria Embankment
☎ 031 337 6707 🌐 www.roma.co.za
⏱ Mon–Sat 6–10 and Fri, Sat noon–2:30

MIDLANDS & UKHAHLAMBA-DRAKENSBERG

Bingelela Contemporary Classic Restaurant RR

Probably the best eatery in the Northern Berg, Bingelela is tucked away in a shady copse between Royal Natal National Park and the small town of Bergville. In an immense thatched construction complete with swimming pool, it has an imaginative menu dominated by the steak and trout, as well as a selection of excellent pizzas, cooked in a wood-fired pizza oven.

☩ 225 D5
✉ R74 about 4km (3mi) north of Bergville
☎ 036 448 1336
🌐 www.bingelela.co.za
⏱ Mon–Sat 7am–10pm, Sun 7–3

Moorcroft Manor RR

A boutique country hotel, set beside a tranquil dam and with great mountain views, which has a relaxed and shady terrace restaurant. Start your day with a buffet breakfast, enjoy lunch of salmon and Camembert salad or ploughman's platter, and for dinner choose from grilled sole, crispy duck or fresh trout. Moorcroft Manor restaurant is also open to non-residents of the hotel.

☩ 225 D4
✉ Sani Road, Himeville
☎ 033 702 1967
🌐 www.moorcroft.co.za
⏱ Daily 7:30–8:30

Rosehurst R

This lovely little café, housed in a red brick Victorian building, is surrounded by a wonderful, fragrant garden full of rose bushes. You can sit in the sun on the terrace for breakfasts of light scrambled eggs, delicious home-made breads, scones and jams, and frothy cappuccinos, or come for the light lunch menu with a Mediterranean feel featuring roasted vegetables, quiches and salads.

☩ 225 D4
✉ 239 Boom Street, Pietermaritzburg
☎ 033 394 3833
⏱ Mon–Fri 8:30–4:30, Sat 8:30–1:30

Yellowwood Café R

Set in an attractive 1870s farmhouse with polished wooden floors, fireplaces, crooked windows and a pretty garden with views of Howick Falls, this child-friendly café and pub serves up an ever-changing menu of hearty, country-style cuisine. Full meals include tender lamb shanks and melt-in-the-mouth oxtail, while the pub menu has lighter meals, and tea and cake is served in the afternoons. For children there is a Kids Menu as well as different birthday party packages with food, drink and jumping castles.

☩ 225 D4
✉ 1 Shafton Road, Howick
☎ 033 330 2461
🌐 www.yellowwood.co.za
⏱ Tue–Sun 8–4:30, Fri, Sat until 8pm

Where to...Shop

DURBAN

The <u>Gateway</u> (M12, Umhlanga Rocks; tel: 031 514 0500; www.gatewayworld. co.za) is one of the largest malls in the southern hemisphere with more than 400 shops, 60 restaurants and fast food outlets and many other recreational facilities. Most international brands are represented here, as well as the local chain stores.

The <u>Pavilion</u> (N3, Westville; tel: 031 275 9800; www.thepav.co.za) is popular, particularly with Indian families and has giant hypermarkets selling just about everything.

The <u>Musgrave Centre</u> (115 Musgrave Road, Berea; tel: 031 201 5129; www. musgravecentre.co.za) has upmarket boutiques and holds a craft-and-curio market in the parking area on Sundays.

In the city centre, the <u>Workshop</u> (99 Samora Machel Street; tel: 031 304 9894; www.theworkshopcentre.co.za) is housed in a restored 1860 industrial building that used to serve as a railway station workshop and is now home to dozens of cheap shops and counters where you can buy Indian snacks. Like most of the larger shopping centres, there is also a multi-screen cinema with the latest international film releases.

Out of town, the <u>Valley of 1,000 Hills</u> is dotted with craft and cottage furniture shops.

There are several markets in Durban and the central <u>Victoria Street Market</u> (155 Victoria Street; tel: 031 306 4021) is a bustling Indian market, where the scents of incense mingle with curries, spices and the odours of the fish market next door; colourful saris, brassware and trinkets are on display.

At the <u>Warwick Triangle</u> adjoining the Victoria Street Market is the <u>Muti Market</u>. Not for the faint-hearted, it should be visited with a guide to help avoid petty crime. Traditional healers sell pungent mixtures of indigenous herbs, plants, bark,

The Indian-influenced Victoria Street Market in Durban sells all manner of spices

The BAT Centre has art galleries, a theatre and music studios, as well as a restaurant and bar where you can relax

snake skins, bird wings, crocodile teeth, dolphin skulls and monkey paws.

For African crafts and curios go to the Amphitheatre flea market held on Sunday mornings on the beachfront (corner Old Fort Road/Snell Parade; tel: 031 301 3200; 9am–4pm).

The Essenwood Craft Market in Berea (Essenwood Road; tel: 081 370 7577; Sat 9–2) is popular with families and offers plenty of craft stalls along with farmers selling fresh produce. The children's playground is conveniently situated so parents can easily keep an eye on them.

West of Durban's centre is the Shongweni Farmer's & Craft Market (Mr551 Road, Outer West Durban; tel: 083 777 4686; www.shongwenimarket.co.za; Sat 6am–11:30am) an authentic farmer's market with stalls of farm fresh food, delicious cakes, bread, jams and much more.

For contemporary African art, pay a visit to the artists' studios in the BAT Centre (Victoria Embankment; tel: 031 332 0451; www.batcentre.co.za) and look out for Zulu beadwork and jewellery, woven baskets, wooden carvings, drums and soapstone figures from Zimbabwe.

MIDLANDS & UKHAHLAMBA-DRAKENSBERG

Many towns in the Drakensberg/Battlefields region have their own arts and crafts routes. The Midlands Meander (tel: 033 330 8195; www.midlandsmeander.co.za), which extends some 80km (50mi) along the country lanes between Pietermaritzburg and Mooi River, is perhaps one of the most popular routes. There are shops and galleries for a whole range of artists, potters, leather workers, furniture makers, blacksmiths, cheese makers and brewers. As well as a good range of restaurants and places to stay along the way.

In the Central Berg visit the Thokozisa Village on the R600, 13km (8mi) west of Winterton, (tel: 036 488 1207; www.cdic.co.za/thokozisa.htm), a one-stop complex gathering together craft shops, art galleries, a deli, restaurant and nursery.

Also worth a visit is the Rorke's Drift Arts and Crafts Centre (tel: 034 642 1627; www.centre-rorkesdrift.com) next to the museum at the Rorke's Drift battle site, 42km (26mi) southeast from Dundee, which specializes in beautiful hand-woven tapestries, pottery and silkscreen fabrics.

Where to...Go Out

CINEMA & THEATRE

Large cinema complexes can be found in the shopping malls, and Durban's Gateway mall has 12 screens alone, along with an indoor climbing wall, skate park and a man-made surfing wave.

Durban's premier theatre is the Playhouse, which also offers backstage tours (231 Anton Lembede Street; tel: 031 369 9555; www.playhousecompany.com).

The Elizabeth Sneddon Theatre (Mazisi Kunene Road, Glenwood; www.sneddontheatre.co.za) is part of the university's drama department and stages a wide variety of shows and music reviews.

Other theatres include the BAT Centre (Victoria Embankment; tel: 031 332 0451; www.batcentre.co.za) and the Catalina Theatre (Wilson's Wharf, Victoria Embankment; tel: 031 837 5999).

The Rhumbelow Theatre (Cunningham Avenue, Umbilo; tel: 031 205 7602; www.rhumbelow.za.net) is a venue for revues; there's a bar and you can take a picnic.

NIGHTLIFE

Durban's casinos are large glitzy affairs. The Sibaya Casino (1 Sibaya Road, Umhlanga; tel: 031 580 5000; www.sun international.com/sibaya) has a theatre and a show bar.

The Suncoast Casino (Marine Parade; tel: 031 328 3000; www.tsogosun.com) has a beach, boardwalk, cinema, water-slide park and several restaurants and bars.

Florida Road in Morningside and Musgrave Road in Berea offer a good selection of venues.

Jazzy Rainbow (93 Smiso Nkwanyana, Morningside; tel: 031 303 8398) is a chic jazz venue featuring live bands.

Its namesake, the Rainbow Restaurant (23 Stanfield Lane; tel: 031 702 9161; www.therainbow.co.za) is an institution in the local jazz scene.

For a more relaxed drink to a musical backdrop of reggae and other Caribbean sounds, head to Cool Runnings (49 Milne Street; tel: 084 701 6912).

In Pietermaritzburg, La Casa (5 Quarry Road; tel: 082 873 7372) presents live music every Tuesday and Friday night.

Dancing and partying in Durban's lively bars and clubs

The Johannesburg skyline in the distance with the
FNB Stadium in the foreground

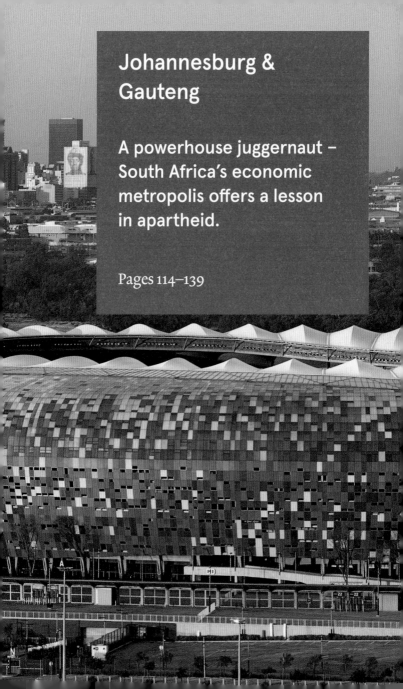

Johannesburg & Gauteng

A powerhouse juggernaut – South Africa's economic metropolis offers a lesson in apartheid.

Getting Your Bearings

Johannesburg is the capital of Gauteng, the smallest province in the country but due to its legacy of gold, also the richest. Until a few years ago the city centre was plagued by crime and much of the action moved to the suburbs. The area has since experienced an urban renewal and, now that it is cleaner and safer, businesses are returning.

The Greater Johannesburg area covers more than 500 suburbs sprawled over 1,300km² (500mi²), which makes it the largest metropolitan region in southern Africa in size, though not in population, which is about 4.4 million. A ribbon of development, the N1 highway and the Gautrain rail link, join Johannesburg to the country's capital Pretoria, 50km (30mi) to the north.

Johannesburg's city centre is dense with high-rises, further out is the township of Soweto, which played a crucial part in the struggle against apartheid. The attractive leafy northern suburbs are where most hotels can be found, as well as superb restaurants, vast shopping malls, glitzy casino resorts, lovely parks and the Johannesburg Zoo.

TOP 10
8 ★★ Pretoria
9 ★★ Soweto

Don't Miss
34 Johannesburg

At Your Leisure
35 Lion Park
36 Cradle of Humankind
37 Lesedi Cultural Village
38 Cullinan Diamond Mine
39 Tswaing Crater

My Day
in the Shadow of
Apartheid

Even though apartheid laws no longer determine the daily lives of South Africans, they are not forgotten and – regrettably – they have also not been completely overcome. Johannesburg is the right place for an examination of South Africa's past and its present. Township tours, restaurant reservations and jazz club tickets should all be booked in advance to avoid disappointment.

8am: Safe Cycling

Start with an early breakfast, as you will be collected at 9am from the Once in Joburg hotel (90 De Korte Street; tel: 087 057 2638; https://once.travel/cities/joburg/) in Braamfontein and taken by shuttle to Soweto (www.sowetobackpackers.com; 2 hours R515). Before you set out on your bike to explore Soweto, the Soweto Backpackers guide will provide you with a cycle helmet and explain what to look out for and remember that Soweto is a big city with big city traffic, so keep an eye out while you're sightseeing.

10am: Township Sightseeing – is it an Option?

The first stop is an old hostel for migrant workers, where the cramped conditions are quite shocking. The tour then visits the Hector Pieterson Memorial that commemorates the

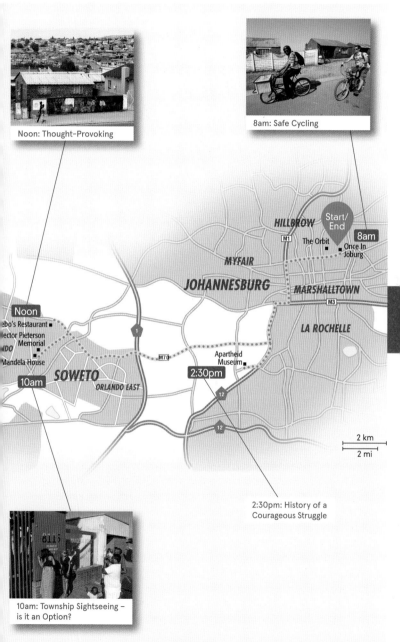

Noon: Thought-Provoking

8am: Safe Cycling

HILLBROW

Start/End

M1

The Orbit

Once In Joburg

8am

MYFAIR

JOHANNESBURG

MARSHALLTOWN

M3

LA ROCHELLE

Noon

ebo's Restaurant

lector Pieterson Memorial

IDO

Mandela House

10am

SOWETO

ORLANDO EAST

1

M70

2:30pm

Apartheid Museum

12

12

2 km

2 mi

2:30pm: History of a Courageous Struggle

10am: Township Sightseeing – is it an Option?

The Hector Pieterson Memorial displays the picture that went all around the world –
1976 student uprising in Soweto

1976 Soweto uprising where Hector Pieterson, a 12-year-old student, was shot dead. This act led to the apartheid regime being condemned by the UN. No tour of Soweto would be complete without a visit to Mandela House on Vilakazi Street – the humble abode of the country's first freely elected president. Desmond Tutu also lived just a few blocks away – two Nobel Peace Prize laureates in a single street!

Noon: Thought-Provoking
Next up is a visit to a market followed by a stop at a *sheebeen* (township pub) for some home-brewed beer, which concludes the cycle tour.

Well hydrated, the group then heads to Lebo's Restaurant for a lunch of typical local dishes such as curry or *mieliepap* (corn porridge). After that, the shuttle takes you back to Johannesburg and then you can take some time to reflect on your township experience. What kind place is Soweto? What do you think of its residents? You may not have seen abject poverty but did you see many white people? Indirectly, apartheid lives on.

2:30pm: History of a Courageous Struggle
A visit to the Apartheid Museum (www.apartheidmuseum.org) immediately confronts the past,

2:30pm

Noon

Above right: In the Apartheid Museum
Below right: Daily life at a market in Soweto

as visitors are arbitrarily assigned a racial classification when purchasing a ticket and then have to use the entrance door for "white" or "non-white", and the latter is considerably shabbier than the former. Once inside, you need strong nerves, not for the really excellent and educational exhibits, but for the individual installations that deliver an emotional punch, such as the hangman's ropes used to execute resistance fighters and the footage of Soweto's protesting students being brutally beaten by the police.

6pm: Upbeat Evening

This is a good time to enjoy an early Afro-European fusion dinner in The Orbit Bistro (81 De Korte Street; tel: 011 339 6645; www.theorbit.co.za), as the evening jam sessions get underway at 8pm. All the big names in the township jazz scene play at The Orbit Jazz Club (admission about R120, depending on the band). You can really relax and let yourself get carried away as you don't need to worry about getting home safely because your hotel is diagonally opposite the venue.

❽ ★★ Pretoria

Don't Miss	South Africa's charming administrative capital
Why	Gracious colonial architecture, leafy parks and interesting museums
Time	One to two days
When	In November when the city's 50,000 jacaranda trees create a beautiful purple haze
What Else	See the famous Mrs Ples
Souvenir	The fragrance of jacaranda blossoms

Tshwane's Church Square with the Paul Kruger Monument by Anton van Wouw

With attractive jacaranda-lined streets and imposing government and historical buildings, Pretoria is South Africa's capital and is steeped in history from the Voortrekker period. It's joined to Johannesburg, 50km (30mi) to the south, by a ribbon of development and green-belt towns along the N1, and it's estimated in another decade or so the area will be one mega-city.

When the Cape became a British colony the descendants of the early Dutch settlers left with their ox wagons and sought new land in the interior. Many put down their roots in the region that is now Pretoria (Tshwane), and the first church was built in 1854, streets were laid out and Pretoria was declared the official capital of the independent Voortrekker republic of Transvaal in 1860. The city was named after Voortrekker leader, Andries Pretorius (1798–1853).

After the Anglo-Boer War, Pretoria was named the capital of the new British colony when the Union of South Africa was created in 1910. Soon after, the renowned architect Herbert Baker built the imposing Union Buildings in Arcadia to the east of the centre. Today, the magnificent complex, in a commanding position on top of a hill, still serves as the seat of South Africa's government. Nelson Mandela made his 1994 inaugural presidential speech in front of it. The buildings are not open to the public so the best reason to come here is to

stroll through the manicured gardens, where there are statues of South Africa's famous generals and an outstanding view of the city. Also in Arcadia, the Pretoria Art Museum is in a light and airy building with an adjoining sculpture park and displays a fine collection of South African art by artists such as Pierneef, Frans Oerder and Anton van Wouw, as well as a collection of old Dutch and Flemish paintings. The nearby 80ha (198-acre) National Zoological Gardens has spacious enclosures that are home to over 2,500 animals. There's a cableway across the two attractions, you can rent golf buggies to get around and there are 6km (4mi) of trails with picnic sites.

The city's main thoroughfare is the 26km-long (16mi) Church Street, which is intercepted by Church Square – the

Pretoria's city centre has returned to life after years of decline

Left: Historic Melrose House, overlooking Burgers Park
Below left: Whale skeleton at the entrance to the National Museum of Natural History
Below: A street lined with jacaranda trees in full bloom

city's first market place and churchyard. Historic buildings surround the square, in the north is the Palace of Justice and the South African Reserve Bank building (designed by Herbert Baker), in the south is the old Raadsaal (council chamber) of the 1891 neo-Renaissance-style Zuid-Afrikaansche Republiek. The Kruger Museum on Church Street served as the residence for president Paul Kruger.

The National Museum of Natural History opposite Pretoria City Hall (Paul Kruger Street) documents the county's natural heritage with exhibits of mammals, reptiles and fossils as well as geological and archaeological finds, including the skull fragment known as Mrs Ples (*Australopithecus africanus*) found at the Sterkfontein Caves, now a UNESCO World Heritage Site (Cradle of Humankind p. 132). Overlooking Burgers Park is Melrose House, which is where the Treaty of Vereeniging was signed in 1902 to end the Anglo-Boer War

(1899–1902). The house was headquarters for the British forces during the war and is today an elegant building with Victorian and Edwardian architectural styles and interiors. The pretty grounds are used for occasional craft fairs and classical concerts.

South of the city there are two imposing buildings. The first is the enormous concrete monstrosity of UNISA, South Africa's largest university. The second is the looming granite Voortrekker Monument on Monument Hill, which was built in 1949 to celebrate the Great Trek and associated wars fought by the Boers in the early to mid-19th century. The bas-relief frieze on the inside has 27 panels depicting the story of the Great Trek. The cenotaph has an opening through which the sun shines at noon on 16 December each year and illuminates the Afrikaans phrase meaning "We for thee, South Africa". It was on 16 December 1838 that the Boers defeated the Zulus in the Battle of Blood River, and under the apartheid government the date was taken as a public holiday, called the Day of the Covenant. Today, 16 December is still a public holiday but has been renamed Day of Reconciliation, with different reasons for celebration.

INSIDER TIP The stables at **Melrose House** have been converted into a delightful **tea garden** with wrought-iron furniture serving light meals, cakes, tea, coffee and wine.

✛ 228 C3

Tshwane Tourist Information Centre
✉ Church Street, Old Nederlandsche Bank Building ☎ 012 358 1430
🌐 www.gopretoria.co.za, www.tshwanetourism.com
◑ Mon–Fri 9–5, Sat until 1pm

Pretoria Art Museum
✉ Arcadia Park ☎ 012 358 6750
🌐 www.pretoriaartmuseum.co.za
◑ Tue–Sun 10–5 🌿 R22

National Zoological Gardens of South Africa
✉ 232 Boom Street ☎ 012 339 2700
🌐 www.nzg.ac.za ◑ Daily 8:30–5:30
🌿 R110

Kruger Museum
✉ 60 WF Nkomo Street ☎ 012 492 5746
🌐 www.ditsong.org.za ◑ Tue–Sat 8:30–4:30, Sun 9–4:30 🌿 R60

National Museum of Natural History
✉ 423 Paul Kruger Street
☎ 012 322 7632 🌐 www.ditsong.org.za
◑ 8–4 🌿 R30

Melrose House
✉ 275 Jeff Masemola Street
(entrance at 280 Scheiding Street)
☎ 012 322 2805 ◑ Tue–Sun 10–5 🌿 22

Voortrekker Monument
✉ Eeufees Road ☎ 012 326 6770
🌐 www.vtm.org.za
◑ May–Aug 8–5; Sep–Apr 8–6 🌿 R70

❾ ★★ Soweto

Don't Miss	Visual legacy of apartheid
Why	Johannesburg's township is a city in its own right
Time	Half a day to a day
When	It is best not to go after dark
What Else	A visit to a *shebeen*
Souvenir	A bucket hat from the street wear brand Thesis Lifestyle

Soweto – short for South Western Township – lies 15km (9mi) southwest of Johannesburg city centre. It gained the world's attention during the 1976 Soweto Uprising when school children, protesting against the introduction of Afrikaans as the language of instruction, sparked a nationwide wave of resistance.

Mahatma Gandhi said: "If we want to achieve true peace in the world, we must begin with the children" and this is still relevant in today's Soweto

Today, with an estimated 1.3 to 2 million inhabitants (almost exclusively black and coloured), Soweto is the largest township in South Africa. A seemingly endless sea of small boxy houses (a few rooms, kitchen and bath), with the less privileged living in crudely built corrugated iron shacks. The residents of Soweto come from all of the indigenous groups found in the country, although Zulus predominate (almost 33 per cent). Nowadays signs of change are evident: well-maintained streets, attractive houses and a golf course. But, while hundreds of kindergartens and schools have been built, there are still not enough, and the only hospital is the massive Chris Hani Baragwaneth Hospital. Mirroring much of the country, the social gulf between white and black has shifted to a gulf between the rich and the poor. As there are hardly any jobs in Soweto, most have to commute to Johannesburg for work. Most areas of Soweto have

Soweto has grown from about 50 small settlements into a huge suburb

electricity and there are some tarred roads but the lack of infrastructure remains striking.

Soweto's struggle against, and the triumph over, apartheid have made it a tourist attraction. More than 1,000 people visit daily on well-organized township tours (bus, walking and cycle tours are available). A tour itinerary usually includes a visit to Mandela House, the excellent Hector Pieterson Museum and Memorial and the Regina Mundi Catholic Church. If you want to get to know Soweto better, you can stay over in one of the welcoming guest houses or in private lodging, which range from simple B&Bs to five-star accommodation. It is best not to drive alone in Soweto as the lack of street names and landmarks makes it hard to navigate. There are surprisingly few criminal incidents involving tourists (especially during the day) but it is advisable to remain vigilant.

INSIDER TIP Choose a tour that includes lunch at **Wandie's Place**, which serves up hearty township cuisine (618 Makhalamele Street, Dube; tel: 081 420 6051; www.wandies.co.za).

✝ 228 C3

Soweto Tourism
✉ Walter Sisulu Square, Kliptown
☎ 011 342 4316
🕐 Mon–Fri 8–5

Mandela House
✉ Ngakane Street, Orlando
☎ 011 936 7754 🌐 www.mandelahouse.com
🕐 Mon–Sun 9–5
🎟 R60

Hector Pieterson Museum and Memorial
✉ 8287 Khumalo Street, Orlando, West Soweto
☎ 011 536 0611
🕐 Mon–Sat 10–5, Sun 10–4 🎟 R30

❸❹ Johannesburg

Don't Miss	A city that conveys the depression, awakening and vision of the new South Africa
Why	Markets, cultural projects and the Apartheid Museum
Time	One to two days
When	Avoid after dark
What Else	A glittering observation deck
In Short	Marvel at the fast-paced development of South African society

Johannesburg, known locally as Jo'burg by the whites and as eGoli by the blacks, is one of the largest cities in Africa. Despite its problems – which continue even through apartheid is over – Johannesburg remains the best place to experience the true buzz of an African city in South Africa.

On the Highveld the Greater Johannesburg metropolitan area, with Pretoria in the north and Vanderbijlpark and Vereeniging in the south, is growing into one endless urban sprawl. Together they form the province of Gauteng, which accounts for only two per cent of the South African state but is home to 22 per cent of the population. The city centre is hemmed in and its architectural charms are rather limited, with a grid layout and high-rise buildings that give it an American feel. Johannesburg has a reputation when it comes to crime, but if you take some sensible precautions your visit should be without incident. Don't carry valuables and avoid quiet side streets. Seek advice from locals about the areas to avoid and stay away from Hillbrow and Yeoville unless you are with a guide. For guided tours try Imbizo Tours: tel: 011 838 2667; http://imbizotours.co.za or Moafrika Tours: tel: 072 783 9787; www.sowetotour.co.za.

Jo'burg's Heartbeat

The streets in the vibrant Newtown district, east of the M1 and around the central Mary Fitzgerald Square, are filled with cafés, galleries, flea markets and music clubs. At Lilian Ngoyi (formerly Bree) the Market Theatre Complex has three performance stages and a craft market outside. Next door

MuseuMAfricA tells the history of Johannesburg since the gold mining days. On the opposite side of the square, at Jeppe Street in Newtown Park is the Workers' Museum where exhibits are dedicated to the migrant labour that came to the city to work in the mines. East of the park is the World of Beer run by South African Breweries, which tells the history of beer and takes you through the brewing process in the greenhouse. There's also a mock-up of a township *shebeen* (pub).

Nearby on Diagonal Street the Museum of Man and Science is actually a shop selling paraphernalia for *sangomas* (traditional healers) and stocks all kinds of ingredients, from plants to animal parts. It's a compelling sight – though the smells may send your senses reeling.

North of Newtown the impressive 284m (931ft) Nelson Mandela Bridge links the city centre with Braamfontein. It spans 42 railway lines and became an iconic symbol of reconciliation after the end of apartheid. In Braamfontein, Constitutional Hill is on the site of the notorious Old Fort Prison complex, also known as Number Four, where blacks were kept in harsh conditions in overcrowded and dirty cells. It has now been converted into a fascinating museum and you can hear stories about some of its most famous inmates such as Nelson Mandela and Mahatma Gandhi.

Panoramic views from the Carlton Centre

Next door is the <u>Constitutional Court</u>. To the east of the city is the 223m-high (730ft), 50-floor <u>Carlton Centre</u> where you can ride a rapid lift up to the <u>Top of Africa</u>, and take in the fabulous views of the busy skyline.

<u>Gold Reef City</u> is based at the top of the 3,293m-deep (10,800ft) Shaft Number 14. The mine opened in 1897 and closed in 1971 and produced 1.4 million kilograms (3.08 million pounds) of gold. You can go down into the shaft where you get a feel of how tough working conditions were for the miners. Above ground is a reconstruction of the mining town. You can be entertained by street performers and have fun on the 30 rides in the adjoining theme park. Not to be missed is the outstanding <u>Apartheid Museum</u>. At the entrance to the museum are pillars representing the seven fundamental principles of South Africa's constitution: democracy, equality, reconciliation, diversity, responsibility, respect and freedom.

INSIDER TIP Treat yourself to a snack or meal in one of the cafés and restaurants in the **Newtown Junction Mall**, north of MuseuMAfricA.

 ✛ 228 C3

Johannesburg Tourism
✉ Park City Transit Centre, Jo'burg Station (corner Rissik/Wolmarans Street), 1st Floor ☎ 011 338 5051
⊕ www.joburgtourism.com
◑ Mon–Fri 8–5

MuseuMAfricA
✉ 121 Lilian Ngoyi Street
☎ 011 833 5624 ◑ Tue–Sun 9–5
➶ Free

Workers' Museum
✉ 52 Rahima Moosa Street
☎ 011 492 0600 ◑ Tue–Sun 9–4:30
➶ Free

World of Beer
✉ 15 Helen Joseph Street, Newtown ☎ 011 836 4900
⊕ www.worldofbeer.co.za
◑ Daily 10–6, tours start hourly on the hour ➶ R125

Museum of Man and Science
✉ 14 Diagonal Street ☎ 011 836 4470
◑ Mon–Fri 7:30–5, Sat 7:30–1 ➶ Free

Constitutional Hill
✉ 1 Kotze Street ☎ 011 381 3100
⊕ www.constitutionhill.org.za
◑ 9–5 ➶ R65–R85

Top of Africa
✉ Carlton Centre, 150 Commissioner Street ☎ 011 308 1331
◑ Mon–Fri 9–6, Sat 9–5, Sun 9–2 ➶ R15

Gold Reef City
✉ Northern Parkway, Ormonde
☎ 011 248 6800 ⊕ www.goldreefcity.co.za ◑ Tue–Sun 9:30–6
➶ R210, children: R130

Apartheid Museum
✉ Northern Parkway, Ormonde
☎ 011 309 4700
⊕ www.apartheidmuseum.org
◑ 9–5 ➶ R85

Meeting Mrs Ples

The grass-covered tumulus of the Cradle of Humankind's Maropeng Visitor Centre (p. 132) is truly imposing. Inside there are a number of interactive exhibits, starting with a theme park-style boat ride (wafts of dry ice mist, erupting volcanoes) that takes you through the earth's history. Then comes the original fossil display covering the story of humankind, where you'll see fascinating human fossils that are up to three million years old. When you stand in front of the replica skull of Mrs Ples, you are looking at one of your most ancient human ancestors.

At Your Leisure

35 Lion Park

A popular day trip destination, the Lion Park is 23km (14mi) north of Johannesburg on the R55. There are two restaurants, shopping facilities and a supervised playground. You can drive through yourself, go on a guided safari from the parking area, or arrange a visit from Johannesburg with one of the tour operators.

The Sterkfontein caves are one of the most significant sites for hominid fossils

✝ 228 C3
✉ M34, near Lanseria Airport
☎ 087 150 0100
🌐 www.lion-park.com
◑ Mon–Fri 8:30am–9pm
💰 From R195

36 Cradle of Humankind

A UNESCO World Heritage Site, the Cradle of Humankind covers almost 500km² (195mi²) about 40km (25mi) to the west of Johannesburg, and is the location of dozens of palaeontological sites that have yielded more human fossils than anywhere else in the world. These sites include the caves of Sterkfontein, Swartkrans, Kromdraai and the surrounding area. In 1947 the skull of an *Australopithecus africanus* was discovered, the first bipedal human ancestor, who populated southern Africa and the Great Rift Valley more than 3 million years ago. The age of the skull is estimated to be 2.6 million years old. Scientists nicknamed it Mrs. Ples but it is now believed to have been a male, roughly 150cm (4.9ft) tall, weighing 35–60kg (77–130lbs) and about 22 years old. In 1997 palaeontologists found the near complete skeleton of another prehistoric man (Little Foot), who lived 3.5 million years ago. Discoveries like these confirm Charles Darwin's theory that the transition from apes to humans took place here in Africa (www.cradleofhumankind.co.za).

Maropeng is a fabulous interactive exhibition, about 10km (6mi) from Sterkfontein, which begins with a boat ride through icebergs, volcanoes and mists demonstrating how the earth and its continents were formed by gases. It then takes visitors on a journey through the story of mankind to the present time. It covers the emergence of man, globalization, population and the effects humans have had on the world and its resources. Each of the exhibits is interactive; you can pick up a phone and listen to the voice of an extinct animal or build up DNA blocks, for example.

✠ 228 C3
✉ Maropeng is on the D400 about 50km (30mi) west of Johannesburg; Sterkfontein is 10km (6mi) away off the R563 ☎ 014 577 9000
🌐 www.maropeng.co.za
🕐 9–5 🎫 Combination tickets for both sites: R190

37 Lesedi Cultural Village

Head here if you want to witness some of southern Africa's tribal customs. There are fully working Zulu, Xhosa, Basotho, Pedi and Sotho mock-up villages that demonstrate traditional tribal living. The programme begins with a presentation on the history and origins of South Africa's rainbow nation. Lunch or dinner is included depending on the tour and both are accompanied by singing and dancing. You can stay overnight in comfortable traditional homesteads, which are grouped in villages (Zulu, Xhosa, Nguni, Basotho, Pedi and Ndebele) hosted by local families.

✠ 228 C3
✉ R512 toward Hartbeespoort
☎ 082 524 45 49 🌐 www.aha.co.za/lesedi
🕐 7am–8:30pm; guided tours at 11:30 and 4:30 🎫 R310 (R575 including lunch)

38 Cullinan Diamond Mine

In 1903, this mine was the source of the Star of Africa, the largest gem diamond ever unearthed, which was presented to King Edward VII for his 66th birthday. The 3,106-carat sparkler was cut into nine major pieces – the largest of which is set as the main stone in the Sceptre of the British monarchy's Crown Jewels – and 96 smaller ones. The mine – which is still operational – can be visited on a tour that includes a viewpoint over the immense hole formed by the original diggings.

✠ 228 C3 ✉ 30km (18mi) east of Pretoria along the R513
ℹ Surface tours can be booked at:
Premier Diamond Tours ☎ 012 734 0081
🌐 www.diamondtourscullinan.co.za, and
Cullinan Tours ☎ 012 734 0260
🌐 www.cullinan-tours.co.za. Cullinan Tourism and History helps booking underground tours ☎ 012 734 2170; www.cullinantourismandhistory.co.za
🎫 Surface tours (2hrs): R170. Underground tours (4hrs): about R500

39 Tswaing Crater

The most impressive scenic attraction in Gauteng, this 1.4km-wide (1mi) and 200m-deep (700ft) crater was created about 220,000 years ago when a meteorite crashed to earth. The Setswana name Tswaing (meaning "Place of Salt") refers to a saline lake on the crater floor. Protected in a small nature reserve, the crater can be circled on foot in around two hours.

✠ 228 C3 ✉ Approximately 35km (21mi) north of Pretoria on the M35
☎ 073 661 5014 🌐 www.ditsong.org.za
🕐 Daily 7:30–4 🎫 R25

Where to...Stay

Expect to pay in high season per double room per night

R   under R1,500
RR   R1,500–R3,000
RRR   over R3,000

JOHANNESBURG

54 on Bath Rosebank RRR
If you are looking for a luxury hotel in a central location then look no further. Formerly known as The Grace in Rosebank, this hotel is close to the Rosebank Mall and has 73 exclusive rooms and 3 suites. All the rooms have marble bathrooms, and the ones near the top of the nine-storey building have great city views. There's a gym and library, and on the roof a delightful English-style garden with a stunning long pool.
✚ 228 C3
✉ 54 Bath Avenue, Rosebank
☎ 011 344 8500 ⊕ www.tsogosun.com

African Pride Melrose Arch Hotel RR–RRR
This ultra-stylish modern hotel is in the Melrose Arch business, residential and shopping development. Rooms have designer furniture, flat-screen TVs, DVDs and great bathrooms (complete with rubber ducks and candles). Facilities include a panelled library, bar and an excellent restaurant with outside tables that are set inside as shallow pool.
✚ 228 C3
✉ 1 Melrose Square, Melrose Arch
☎ 011 214 6666
⊕ www.africanpridemelrosearch.com

Backpacker's Ritz R
This is the best of Johannesburg's backpacker hostels, with roomy dorms, neat doubles and a pool in the gardens. The useful travel centre can organize all activities, tours and transport, there's a kitchen for residents and Hyde Park Corner mall is within walking distance. They also run their own affordable day tours using guides from Soweto.
✚ 228 C3
✉ 1A North Road, Dunkeld West
☎ 011 325 7125
⊕ www.backpackers-ritz.com

De Kuilen Country House R
This 5-star guest house has four delightful cottages in Cape Dutch style and one unique tree house in 1ha (3 acres) of peaceful gardens. The French-trained chef presents delicious four-course dinners served on silver, crystal and white linen; there's an extensive wine collection. Beauty treatments are on offer.
✚ 228 C3
✉ 26 Glenluce Drive, Sandton
☎ 011 462 4670 ⊕ www.dekuilen.co.za

Maropeng Boutique Hotel R
Attached to the Maropeng Visitor Centre, this isolated 24-room hotel provides a peaceful, scenic alternative to staying in central Johannesburg, offering spacious accommodation with fine views to the Witwatersrand and Magaliesberg ranges. It is especially convenient for extended exploration of the Cradle of Humankind (p. 132).
✚ 228 C3 ✉ On the D400 about 50km (30mi) west of Johannesburg
☎ 014 577 9100 ⊕ www.maropeng.co.za

Michelangelo Towers RRR
This 5-star hotel in a wonderful location overlooking Nelson Mandela Square. The spacious rooms are elegantly decorated and there's a luxurious turndown service when the room is scattered with rose petals. There is also a heated indoor pool and spa.
✚ 228 C3
✉ 8 Maude Street, Sandton
☎ 011 245 4000 ⊕ www.legacyhotels.co.za

Pablo House R
This affordable boutique guest house in Melville is situated on a ridge and offers uninterrupted views of the city. There are numerous restaurants, bars and a shopping centre in the vicinity. The high-ceilinged rooms are spacious, bright and welcoming.
✚ 228 C3
✉ 3 Fourth Avenue, Mellville
☎ 066 215 0993 ⊕ http://pablohouse.co.za

The Saxon RRR
Tucked away in the leafy northern suburbs and set in a 2.5ha (6-acre) estate with manicured lawns and a vast infinity pool, this

Ten Bompas is located in the suburb of Dunkeld West

boutique hotel was where Nelson Mandela stayed to edit his autobiography when he was released from prison. The luxurious furnishings feature African art and antiques.

✝ 228 C3
✉ 36 Saxon Road, Sandhurst
☎ 011 292 6000 ⊕ www.saxon.co.za

Ten Bompas RRR
With just 10 suites this is a peaceful boutique hotel within walking distance of Hyde Park Corner mall. The modern interior design uses an appealing collection of African art, and each room is individually decorated. The restaurant is superb and there are lots of special touches such as cookies and hot drinks delivered to the rooms.

✝ 228 C3
✉ 10 Bompas Road, Dunkeld West
☎ 011 325 2442 ⊕ www.tenbompas.com

PRETORIA

Cricklewood Manor RRR
The 5-star hotel, set in the sleepy, shady suburb of Waterkloof, only five minutes' drive from central Pretoria, combines luxurious, modern all-suite accommodation with elegant architecture and lovely green grounds. There is also an excellent restaurant and on-site spa.

✝ 228 C3
✉ 193 Albert Street, Waterkloof
☎ 012 460 8225 ⊕ www.cricklewood.co.za

Where to...Eat and Drink

Expect to pay for a two-course meal per person excluding drinks:
R   under R200
RR   R200–R350
RRR over R350

JOHANNESBURG

Browns of Beverly Hills RR
The Brown offers exculsive dining and a cellar with an impressive selection of fine wines. There is afull and varied menu (try the Spatchcock Chicken), some wicked desserts and on Sundays there is spit-roast lamb.

✝ 228 C3
✉ 31 Mulbarton Rd, Lonehill, Sandton
☎ 060 946 9975
⊕ www.brownz.co.za
🕐 Tue–Sat noon–10, Sun noon–3:30

Bukhara RRR
Within the Michelangelo Hotel in Nelson Mandela Square, this is one of the country's top Indian restaurants. The cuisine is authentic and each dish is made from scratch. There's a full range of tikka masala, murg and tandoori dishes.

✝ 228 C3
✉ Nelson Mandela Square, Sandton
☎ 011 883 5555
⊕ www.bukhara.com
🕐 Mon–Sat noon–3, 6–11, Sun 6pm–10pm

The Butcher Shop and Grill RR–RRR

For a tender steak, head to this celebrated steak restaurant. Steaks are cut and cooked to order and served with a variety of sauces and vegetables. Lamb, pork and seafood are also on the menu, but there's not much choice for vegetarians.

✢ 228 C3
✉ Nelson Mandela Square, Sandton
☎ 011 784 8676
⊕ www.thebutchershop.co.za
◑ Daily noon–11

Fourno's Bakery R

This is the northern suburbs' most popular pavement-side spot for breakfast – try the bacon bagels or poached egg and salmon. The in-house bakery turns out fresh bread, cakes, quiches, pies and sausage rolls and the extensive deli counter offers takeaway meals.

✢ 228 C3
✉ Dunkeld West Centre, Jan Smuts Avenue
☎ 011 325 2110
⊕ www.fournos.co.za
◑ Mon–Fri 7–6, Sat 6–6, Sun 7–3

Moyo Melrose Arch RRR

A flamboyant chain of restaurants that offers a combination of fine food from across the African continent, and an excellent range of wines and entertainment. Musicians wander among the tables, ladies wash your hands or give you henna tattoos, the staff are dressed in beautiful African fabrics, and there's always something going on, from Zulu dancing to tap dancing. The food ranges from Moroccan tajines and Tunisian meze, to Mozambique curries and South African seafood. The shop sells some wonderful handcrafted art. Dining here would be a highlight of any trip to Johannesburg and it is hugely popular so make reservations.

✢ 228 C3
⊕ www.moyo.co.za
✉ Melrose Square ☎ 011 684 1477
◑ Daily 11–11
Also at:
✉ Zoo Lake ☎ 011 646 0058
◑ Mon–Thu 8:30am–10pm,
Fri, Sat 8:30am–11pm

Niki's Oasis RR

Niki Sondlo was the first to rediscover the inner city and invest in it. Her jazz club and restaurant is a success story, a Newtown institution that attracts top local and international jazz musicians, and Niki is always on hand to chat about the pictures of cultural icons that line the walls. There is live music on Friday nights and before the music kicks off you can enjoy some traditional food or sandwiches, barbecue chicken, T-bone steaks or burgers. The club attracts the art scene crowd and the hip Jo'burg youth.

✢ 228 C3
✉ 138 Lilian Ngoyi Street, Newtown
☎ 011 838 9733
◑ Daily noon–midnight

Trumps Grillhouse and Butchery R–RR

Located in the heart of the suburb of Sandton, this is seventh heaven for lovers of perfectly aged steaks – the excellent quality meat served here comes from their on-site butchery. And to avoid any confusion about the Trump name, rest assured that the restaurant has been operating under this name since 1994 and is a local Mandela Square institution. Very good value for money.

✢ 228 C3
✉ Nelson Mandela Square, Sandton
☎ 011 784 23 66
⊕ www.trumpsgrill.co.za
◑ Daily 11–10

PRETORIA

O'Galito RR

It's best known for its affordable seafood including sardines, crab, lobster and skewers of queen prawns. Try the oysters with a sauce of shrimps, mushrooms, sherry and parmesan; meat eaters can go for the rabbit in red wine or oxtail with butter beans.

✢ 228 C3
✉ 30A Woodlands Boulevard, Pretoria East
☎ 012 997 4164
⊕ www.ogalito.com
◑ Daily noon–2:30, 6–10

Where to...Shop

SHOPS

In Johannesburg's northern suburbs is the glitzy Sandton City mall (Rivonia Road, Sandton; tel: 011 217 6000; www.sandtoncity. com) and its adjacent piazza-style Nelson Mandela Square, lined with restaurants and with a wonderful atmosphere. This is also where you'll find just about all of the international labels and brands.

Rosebank Mall (Cradock Road; tel: 011 788 5530; www.rosebankmall.co.za) has a good selection of shops.

Of particular interest is also the Rosebank Art & Craft Market selling a wide selection of jewellery, traditional clothing and crafts. The mall has more than 160 tenants including Maple Galleries (antiques and gifts), a post office and a Computicket where you can make bookings for theatre performances or other events.

Other malls include the vast Cresta Mall (Beyers Naude Drive, Northcliff; tel: 011 678 5306; www.crestashoppingcentre.co.za), Hyde Park Corner (Jan Smuts Avenue,

Hyde Park; tel: 011 325 4340; www.hydepark-corner.co.za), which features designer clothing and jewellery stores, and Brightwater Commons (Republic Road, Randburg; tel: 011 886 0663; www.bright watercommons.co.za) where the shops are set amongst attractive lawns and waterfalls.

For a more serious selection of South African art, visit the Everard Read Gallery (6 Jellicoe Avenue, Rosebank; tel: 011 788 4805; www.everard-read.co.za), the Kim Sacks Gallery (153 Jan Smuts Avenue, Parkwood; tel: 011 447 5804; www.kimsacks-gallery.com) and the nearby Goodman Gallery (163 Jan Smuts Ave; tel: 011 788 1113; www.goodman-gallery.com).

For antiques, collectables and homewares head to the shops along Parkhurst's Fourth Avenue. For books, try Exclusive Books (www.exclusivebooks.co.za), with branches in all the malls.

On your Soweto tour, be sure to check out the Thesis Concept Store (173 Machaba Dr, Mofolo, Soweto; tel: 011 982 1182). The store carries trendy streetwear from various Soweto designers as well as their range of iconic bucket hats.

The massive and elegant Sandton City shopping centre is a paradise for serious shopaholics

Johannesburg's diverse shopping malls, and countless boutiques, offer both international brand items and fashion by local designers

MARKETS

The African Craft Market (Cradock Ave, Rosebank) is the best place to shop for African crafts.

Clothing, handicrafts and everything else imaginable (often made in China) can be found at the Bruma Lake Flea Market (Oriental City, corner Ernest Oppenheimer and Marcia avenues, Bruma; Tue–Sun 9:30–5). There is also live entertainment and a wide range of food stalls.

Michael Mount Organic Village Market (Bryanston Road, Bryanston; www.bryanston organicmarket.co.za) offers organic produce and crafts on Thursdays and Saturdays.

The residents of the hip Maboneng Precinct have set up a community street market with Market on Main (corner Sivewright Avenue and Fox Street, http://marketonmain.co.za, 10–3) it takes place every Sunday and offers a vibrant atmosphere and lots of tasty food.

Rosebank Sunday Market (Rosebank Mall, Cradock Road, www.rosebanksundaymarket.co.za; Sun 9–5) is a flea market held on the Rosebank Mall rooftop where you'll find clothing, crafts, collectibles, food stalls and live entertainment.

The Oriental Plaza (38–60 Lilian Ngoyi Street, Fordsburg; www.orientalplaza.co.za; Mon–Fri 9–5, Sat 6–3) is where the Indian traders sell clothing, spices and Indian snacks; it is also open Monday to Saturday.

Where to...Go out

NIGHTLIFE

Montecasino (William Nicol Drive, Fourways; tel: 011 510 7995; www.montecasino.co.za) has a casino, a theatre, several restaurants, cafés and bars, and the Montecasino Bird Garden (tel: 011 511 1864), a unique bird park which has an excellent free-flight show.

Emperor's Palace (64 Jones Street, Kempton Park; tel: 011 928 1000; www.emperorspalace.com) has a casino, theatre, show bar, restaurants and fashionable nightclubs.

Another popular club, the <u>Moon Light Lounge</u> in the <u>Back o' the Moon</u> restaurant is at the <u>Gold Reef City Casino</u> (Northern Parkway Drive, Ormonde; tel: 011 496 1423; www.tsogosun.com), which often features live jazz.

Another excellent jazz venue <u>Bassline</u> (10 Henry Nxumalo Street, Newtown; tel: 011 838 9145; www.basslinejazzclub.co.za) also specializes in Kwaito (South African rap) and hip-hop artists.

<u>Katzy's</u> (corner Oxford Road and Bierman Avenue at The Firs/Hyatt Shopping Centre; tel: 011 880 3945, www.katzys.co.za) is one of Johannesburg's best jazz clubs and also offers over one hundred varieties of whiskies, some excellent cocktails and a plush leather-and-wood interior.

Nightclubs tend to come and go, but popular venues include <u>ESP</u> (84 Oxford Road, Ferndale; tel: 011 792 4110; www.esp. co.za; Sat only).

<u>And Club</u> (39a Gwi Gwi Mrwebi Street, Newtown; Thu–Sat 9pm–4am; www.and club.co.za) is the best venue if you are looking for a party, expect lots of drum and base, house, electro, hip-hop. Check www.inyourpocket.com/johannesburg and www.iol.co.za/tonight for listings.

THEATRE

The large <u>Joburg Theatre Complex</u> (Loveday Street, Braamfontein; tel: 011 877 6800; www.joburgtheatre.com), whose three stages host musicals, ballet and opera, and community or supper theatres showing meaty plays or comedy. To find out what's on and book tickets, visit the Computicket desks or book online (www. computicket.co.za).

<u>Market Theatre</u> (Margaret Mcingana Street, Newtown; tel: 011 832 1641; www. markettheatre.co.za) was an important venue during apartheid for protest theatre.

The <u>Old Mutual Theatre on the Square</u> (Nelson Mandela Square, Sandton; tel: 011 883 8606; www.theatreonthesquare.co.za) is a good venue for comic plays.

There are also several stages at the <u>Wits University Theatre Complex</u> (Jorissen Street, Braamfontein; tel: 011 717 1372; www. wits.ac.za/witstheatre).

The Emperor's Palace is an enormous, opulent hotel and entertainment complex inspired by the famous Las Vegas casinos

Elephant herd and some adorable young calves crossing a river

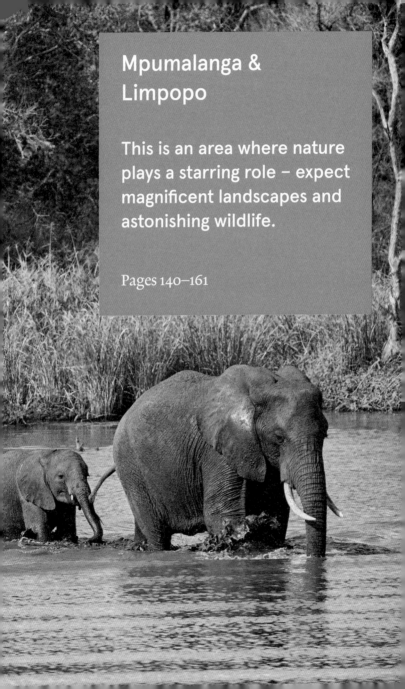

Mpumalanga & Limpopo

This is an area where nature plays a starring role – expect magnificent landscapes and astonishing wildlife.

Pages 140–161

Getting Your Bearings

Limpopo and Mpumalanga, the two northeastern provinces of South Africa, are areas traditionally settled by the Sepedi, Ndebele and Zulu. The land here is wild and unspoiled and that does not just apply to the Kruger National Park. There are also the breathtaking, mountainous landscapes of the Klein Drakensberg escarpment and the Blyde River Canyon. When it comes to exploring the national parks, a private vehicle is an advantage but you can also join one of the organized tours offered by the many tour operators and lodges.

Mbombela, the capital of Mpumalanga, lies on the Crocodile River in the subtropical lowveld. It is the gateway to the Kruger National Park and has good transport links (bus, train and plane). Here in the north nature in its purest form awaits the traveller: South Africa's largest wildlife reserve right next to the tremendous scenery of the acclaimed Blyde River Canyon, South Africa's own Grand Canyon. There are not enough superlatives to describe this beautiful region where you will encounter the passing show of Africa's legendary Big Five, stunning vistas of bizarre erosion sculptures, lush gorges and spectacular waterfalls. Polokwane, the largest city and the capital of Limpopo, is on the N1 highway north of Johannesburg, and serves as a good stopover en route to your safari.

TOP 10
- ❶ ★★ Kruger National Park
- ❻ ★★ Panorama Route

Don't Miss
- ㊵ Kruger Private Game Reserves

At Your Leisure
- ㊶ Barberton
- ㊷ Hoedspruit Endangered Species Centre
- ㊸ Magoebaskloof Pass
- ㊹ Mapungubwe National Park

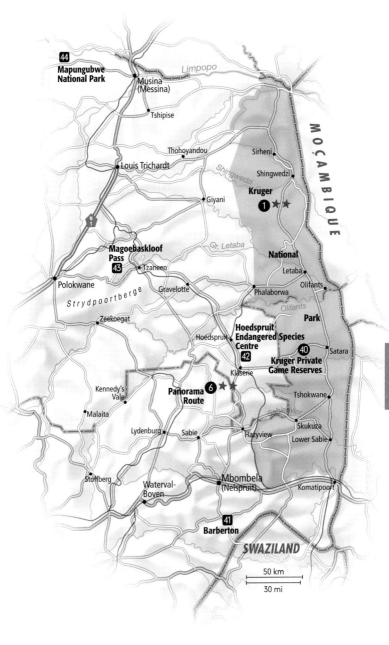

44 Mapungubwe National Park

Musina (Messina)

Limpopo

Tshipise

M O Ç A M B I Q U E

Thohoyandou

Sirheni

Shingwedzi

Louis Trichardt

Shingwedzi

Giyani

Kruger

1 ★★

N1

Gr. Letaba

National

Letaba

Olifants

Magoebaskloof Pass

43

Tzaneen

Gravelotte

Phalaborwa

Olifants

Polokwane

Strydpoortberge

Zeekoegat

Park

Hoedspruit Endangered Species Centre

Hoedspruit

42

Kruger Private Game Reserves

40

Satara

Klaserie

Kennedy's Vale

Panorama Route

6 ★★

Malaita

Tshokwane

Lydenburg

Sabie

Sabiervier

Stoffberg

Hazyview

Skukuza

Lower Sabie

Waterval-Boven

Mbombela (Nelspruit)

Komatipoort

41

Barberton

SWAZILAND

50 km

30 mi

My Day
Among
Wild Animals

This tour of the southern section of the Kruger National Park starts at the Skukuza restcamp, 12km (7.5mi) east of the Paul Kruger Gate. A high-clearance off-road vehicle is recommended and when you arrive at camp, ask about the condition of the park's roads as rainfall can make them impassable. Be sure to book your accommodation for Skukuza (www.krugerpark.co.za) and Rhino Post Safari Lodge well in advance – before your trip to South Africa!

5:30am: Rise And Shine!

Only early risers get to see lions, so check out and set off as soon as the Skukuza gates open and take the S114 (also H1–1) south towards Pretoriuskop. Drive slowly as animals may cross the road at any time, forcing you to stop abruptly (speed limit 40km/h 25mph).

Driving slowly is also the only way that you'll spot the park's game – perfectly camouflaged by the surrounding bushveld – and this area is considered a safe bet for lion sightings. After about 10km (6mi) you can take a short break at the Mathekenyane Koppie. The granite hilltop is a magnificent vantage

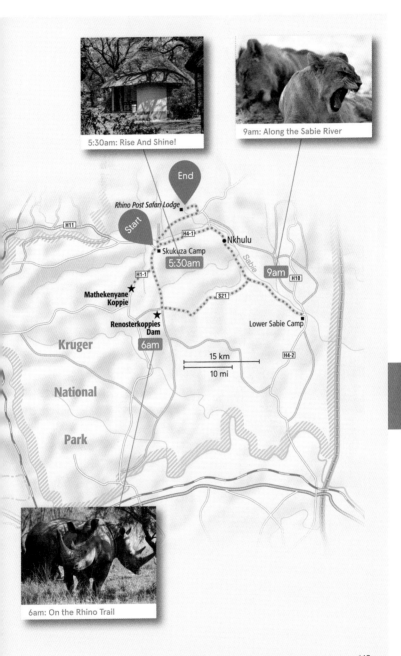

5:30am: Rise And Shine!

9am: Along the Sabie River

End

Rhino Post Safari Lodge

Start

H11

H4-1

Nkhulu

Skukuza Camp
5:30am

Sabie

9am

H10

H1-1

Mathekenyane
Koppie

S21

Renosterkoppies
Dam
6am

Lower Sabie Camp

Kruger

15 km

H4-2

10 mi

National

Park

6am: On the Rhino Trail

MY DAY...

Left: A leopard with its springbok kill
Centre above: On the way to breakfast
Centre below: A lion taking a siesta

point that offers panoramic views over the national park's southern bushveld. You may even spot some giraffes.

🕕 6am: On the Rhino Trail
Drive back to the S114 and follow it south for around 15km (10mi) to the Renosterkoppies Dam, another excellent opportunity for game viewing. There's a granite outcrop where you can watch the game coming and going. It's a favourite

with rhinos and you may see buffalo emerge from the bush, or even the occasional spotted hyena. From here, turn left onto the S21 and you'll soon reach the Sand River, which you continue to follow. Keep your eyes open as the dense bush is the ideal hideout for leopards.

🕗 8am: Breakfast in Nature
After 30km (20mi) you reach the Sabie River, follow it 11km (7mi) to the south and the Lower Sabie

Game viewing in small groups – camera always at the ready

<u>Camp</u> comes into view. The Sabie River is known for having some of the best game viewing in the park – large prides of lions, leopards, rhinos, and herds of elephants, crocodiles and hippos. Afterwards, you can enjoy a breakfast break in the camp restaurant overlooking the river.

🕘 9am: Along the Sabie River
By now it is almost too late for game sightings – certainly for the big cats – as they are all having a siesta. But look out for less sensational creatures, such as tortoises, kudu, meerkats and the colourful birdlife. Continuing north from Lower Sabie Camp, you can hone your game view-ing skills on the 25km (15.5mi) drive along the Sabie River. Take another break on the river at <u>Nkhulu</u>, where you can watch the crocodiles. Then it's another 20km (12.5mi) further along the Sabie River back to <u>Skukuza</u>.

🕒 3pm: Head to the Lodge
Set off for the <u>Rhino Post Safari Lodge</u> (tel: 035 474 1473; www.isibindi.co.za), which lies 20km (12.5mi) to the north. The lodge features luxurious chalets, a pool and game drives that start at around 4:30pm. The drives take about 4 hours and reveal many of the bushveld's secrets. Thereafter, an exquisite dinner concludes your African night in style.

❶ ★★ Kruger National Park

Don't Miss	South Africa's renowned national park with rich reserves of wildlife
Why	Savannah, waterholes, huge herds of game and the Big Five
Time	One to five days
When	In the dry season (June–Oct) when the game is more visible
What Else	In the evening put some *boerewors* on the braai and open an ice-cold beer
In Short	Storybook Africa

The 20,000km² (7,800mi²) park was established in 1898 and is one of Africa's largest reserves. The vast park is bordered by Mozambique to the east, Zimbabwe to the north, and private game reserves to the west. In 2002 the park became one of the so-called Peace Parks when it linked to the Gonarezhou National Park in Zimbabwe and the Limpopo National Park in Mozambique, forming the Great Limpopo Transfrontier Park.

Kruger National Park is one of the richest game reserves in southern Africa. Here you are almost guaranteed to see the Big Five – the 2018 census recorded 1,500 lions, 1,000 leopard 17,000 elephants and 48,000 buffalo – as well 250,000 antelope, 8,000 giraffes and 3,000 crocodiles. There are a total

Pretoriouskop's round huts seen through the bright flowers of a coral tree

Picnic with Crocodiles

In the southern Kruger National Park, on the banks of the Sabie River is Nkuhlu, a tranquil site shaded by the mighty crowns of ancient Natal mahogany trees. Nkuhlu means "place of many big trees" and it is a wonderful picnic spot with sweeping views across the savannah and the river. Sitting here you may see a giant kingfisher plunge into the water like an arrow, a Goliath heron stalking majestically through the mud, or a riverbank rock suddenly move… just a crocodile changing position.

of 147 mammal species, 550 bird species and 114 species of reptiles. The park is also home to about 300 endangered African wild dogs, so if you spot a wild dog or one of the 150 cheetahs, you'll be very lucky.

Leopards can climb trees with a few leaps

Coral or Marula?

The variety of flora is as equally impressive as the fauna. Tracts of mopane woodlands characterise the northern half while the southern region has open veld with scrub, buffalo grass and different species of acacia, coral and marula trees. The parks hot, rainy season is in the summer months from November to April, with a cool dry season in the winter. The best time for game viewing is during the dry season when the bush thins out and animals can easily be spotted congregating along the rivers or waterholes. The southern part, between Sabie and the Olifants River, is more geared towards tourism and has the most camps and lodges. All visitors must leave the park before the gates close in order to allow enough time to travel to the restcamps. These are the most popular camps: Lower Sabie (where numerous buffaloes, elephants, warthogs and lions come to drink at the dam), Pretoriouskop (set in a landscape of enormous granite outcrops and a good place for spotting white rhino), and Olifants, which offers spectacular views of hippo, buffalo, giraffe, kudu, elephant and numerous birds.

Burchell's zebra are the smallest of the zebra species and have the widest stripes

INSIDER TIP Plan your route to reach Letaba at noon. First visit **Letaba Elephant Hall**, a fascinating museum all about elephants, and then head off for lunch in the camp restaurant.

✚ 229 E/F4/5
☎ 012 428 9111 ⊕ www.sanparks.org; www.krugerpark.co.za
◑ Jan–Feb, Nov–Dec 5:30am–

6:30pm; Mar, Oct 5:30am–6pm;
Apr 6am–5:30pm;
May–Aug 6:30am–5:30pm; Sep 6–6
💰 R328

❻ ★★ Panorama Route

Don't Miss	Scenic road with breathtaking viewpoints
Why	Winding mountain passes, dramatic waterfalls, rock sculptures, gold mining settlements and a canyon
Time	One day
When	In the dry season (June–October) you have the best view of the canyon
What Else	Pan for gold like a prospector of yesteryear
Souvenir	With a little luck you may find a gold nugget

The Panorama Route winds its way along rugged mountain passes, past dramatic waterfalls, deep canyons and pictur- esque country towns surrounded by pine and eucalyptus forests. It offers fantastic views from the edge of the Drankensberg escarpment out over of the Kruger National Park's plains 1,000m (3,280ft) below.

Ringed by mountains and vast pine and eucalyptus planta- tions, Sabie was once a small gold mining town. Today it's the centre for the largest man-made forest in the country, which supports an estimated 50 per cent of South Africa's timber needs. The interesting SAFCOL Forest Industry Museum can organize day and overnight hikes and moun- tain biking in the forests. Near town, the Sabie Falls, Bridal Veil Falls, Horseshoe Falls and Lone Creek Falls are well worth a visit and 12km (7mi) of the Sabie River have been reserved for trout fishing. There are more waterfalls around Graskop, another forestry centre with a main street lined with restaurants and gift shops.

Gold Rush Era

To the east, the picturesque village of Pilgrim's Rest has been declared a national monument for its gold mining history: gold was discovered here in 1873. Today the single street of Victorian miners' cottages has been restored to its former glory, and it houses a number of interesting museums for which tickets can be bought at the tourist office. At the Diggings Site you can watch a demonstration

The giraffe's coat pattern provides excellent camouflage

of gold panning and have a go yourself.

God's Window

North of Graskop, en route to <u>Blyde River Canyon</u> are a number of viewpoints with names like "God's Window" and "Wonder View", which hint at views they offer over the lowveld running back towards the Kruger Park. Even more spectacular is the Blyde River Canyon itself, which is one of the largest canyons in Africa at 26km (16mi) long and up to 800m (2,624ft) deep. There are a series of marked hiking trails running through the bottom of the gorge. Another fantastic sight is that of the <u>Three Rondavels</u>: three huge domes of dolomite rock rising out of the far wall, so-named because they resemble traditional, circular African huts. At <u>Bourke's Luck Potholes</u> a network of pathways and footbridges allow you to explore the potholes – strange cylindrical sculptures carved by swirling water at the confluence of the Blyde and Treur rivers. You can continue along the R532 and then the R36 to the bottom of the canyon and further eastwards to <u>Hoedspruit</u> and Kruger's Orpen Gate.

INSIDER TIP Graskop is famous for its pancakes so head straight for **Harrie's Pancakes** (p. 158) on the main street.

ℹ️ ✛ 229 E4

SAFCOL Forest Industry Museum
✉️ 10th Ave, Sabie ☎ 013 754 2724
🌐 www.safcol.co.za 🕐 Mon–Fri
8–4:30, Sat 8–noon 🏷️ R10

Pilgrim's Rest Tourist Information
✉️ Main Street, Pilgrim's Rest
☎ 013 768 10 60

🌐 www.pilgrims-rest.co.za
🕐 Daily 9–12:45, 1:45–4

Diggings Site
✉️ 1km (0.6mi) south of Pilgrim's Rest
🕐 Daily hour-long tours leave at 10, 11, noon, 2 and 3 🏷️ R12

Bourke's Luck Potholes
☎ 013 774 3617 🕐 Daily 7–5 🏷️ R55

⓴ Kruger Private Game Reserves

Don't Miss	The ultimate *Out of Africa* experience
Why	Privately owned game parks offering luxurious lodges and tented camps
Time	One to three nights
When	The dry season (June–October) is the best time for game viewing
What Else	The sound of the African wilderness at night
In Short	The expense is well worth it

In the wide lowveld plains of the southwest border of Kruger Park are numerous private game reserves. They offer exclusive experiences with luxurious accommodation in elegant lodges or in gorgeous safari tents with every comfort.

The 'King of the Beasts' is Africa's largest land predator

Most game reserves charge an admission fee and at some you may also have to pay a small conservation levy at the lodge. On game drives, headed by experienced guides, you will learn about the different species of birds and animals.

INSIDER TIP A normal day on safari begins with coffee and rusks at dawn before an early morning game drive. A late brunch is served back at the lodge and in the evening there is a sumptuous dinner.

✛ 229 E3

Kapama Game Reserve
⊕ www.kapama.co.za

Klaserie Private Nature Reserve
⊕ www.klaseriecamps.com

MalaMala Game Reserve
⊕ www.malamala.com

Manyeleti Game Reserve
⊕ www.manyeleti.co.za

Sabi Sands Game Reserve
⊕ www.sabi-sands.co.za

Thornybush Game Reserve
⊕ www.thornybushcollection.co.za

Timbavati Private Nature Reserve
⊕ www.timbavati.co.za

At Your Leisure

41 Barberton

After the discovery of gold in 1884, a mining town instantly sprang up here. Four years later and Barberton's gold rush was over and prospectors moved on to the richer deposits of the Witwatersrand. Today all that remains of the glory days are a few historical buildings, some of which are open to the public. The Barberton Museum has exhibits on gold, geology, mining and the general history of the region.

✛ 229 E3
✉ Crown Street
☎ 013 712 2880
⊕ www.barberton.co.za
D Mon–Fri 7:30–5, Sat 8–1

42 Hoedspruit Endangered Species Centre

The small town of Hoedspruit, which lies just 30km northwest of the Kruger National Park's Orpen Gate, is home to several wildlife rehabilitation centres, including the Moloholo Wildlife Rehab Centre (www.moholoholo.co.za). One of South Africa's leading breeding and research centres for endangered species, the Hoedspruit Endangered Species Centre, is part of the Kapama Game Reserve (p. 153). The project was initially established to breed cheetah and more than 80 can be seen. The reserve is also home to wild dog, young rhinos, African wild cat, ground hornbills and various antelope. Guided tours depart on the hour: visitors travel in open safari vehicles around the animal enclosures. You can also arrange an elephant ride at the affiliated Camp Jabulani – if you opt to stay overnight at the camp there's the chance to ride an elephant in the dark!

✛ 229 E4
✉ Off the R40, near Hoedspruit
☎ 015 793 1633
⊕ www.hesc.co.za
🕐 Tours daily 9, 11, 1 and 3 🖈 R165

43 Magoebaskloof Pass

From Tzaneen – the centre of a lush agricultural region and a popular stopover on the way to the Kruger National Park – the R71 heads southwest through the Magoebaskloof Pass. The road first runs parallel to the Magoebas River valley then, after about 18km (11mi) there is a right turn and after another 3km (2mi) it takes you to the remote Debegeni Falls. The spectacular waterfall cascades 80m (260ft) down into a small lake, where swimming is allowed. The road continues to climb steeply before reaching the summit (1,400m/ 4,600ft) and the Magoebaskloof Hotel. Further on is the Ebenezer Dam, an excursion area popular for picnics, birding, boating and fishing.

From here it is only 5km (3mi) to Haenertsburg, which is known for its trout and its Spring Festival in September. You can do the relatively easy Magoebaskloof Hiking Trail (starting at De Hoek Forest Station near Tzaneen; tel: 013 754 2724; permit required), a lesser-known hike that leads through lush, indigenous vegetation and picturesque scenery. Six rustic huts along the route provide overnight accommodation.

✛ 229 D4
✉ Haenertsburg
☎ 083 442 7429
🌐 www.magoebaskolooftourism.co.za
⏱ Mon–Fri 8–5, Sat, Sun 8.30–noon

44 Mapungubwe National Park

It is just an unassuming hill in the remote rocky border area of South Africa, Botswana and Zimbabwe,

Baobab tree in Mapungubwe National Park, a UNESCO World Heritage Site since 2003

yet it has provided archaeologists with an entirely different view of the history of Africa. In 1932, archaeologists uncovered graves where the dead wore precious gold jewellery and were buried with grave goods from Arabia and Asia. Mapungubwe Hill revealed traces of a wealthy African trading kingdom that existed before the stone city of Great Zimbabwe, the oldest known southern African culture to date. It is believed that Mapungubwe was at its height from 1050 to the end of the 13th century and traded along the East African coast, where objects from Arabia and China were acquired. In 1994, the government declared the excavation site a national park; in 2002 the then-president, Thabo Mbeki, established the Order of Mapungubwe, South Africa's highest order, and awarded it to Nelson Mandela. In 2003, UNESCO declared the ruins and graves a World Heritage Site. Artefacts that were previously held by the University of Pretoria were returned to the new Interpretive Centre that opened on site in September 2011. Book a guided walking tour of the archaeological hill site at the park's central office.

✛ 229 D5
✉ 70km (42mi) west of Musina on the R572
☎ 015 534 7925
🌐 www.sanparks.org
⏱ Day visitors: Sep–Mar 6am–6:30pm; Apr–Aug 6:30am–6pm 🏷 R192

Where to...Stay

Expect to pay in high season per double room per night

R   under R1,500
RR   R1,500–R3,000
RRR   over R3,000

KRUGER NATIONAL PARK & PRIVATE GAME RESERVES

Camp Jabulani RRR
Under thatch with slate walls and contemporary African furnishings, the six elegant suites have slide-away walls for views of the bush, wooden decks and plunge pools.
✛ 229 E4
✉ Kapama Game Reserve ☎ 015 793 1265 (camp),
012 460 5605 (reservations)
⊕ www.campjabulani.com

MalaMala (Main Camp, Rattray's, Sable Camp) RRR
These are three camps in the 13,000ha (32,123-acre) MalaMala Game Reserve, South Africa's largest privately owned Big Five reserve, which shares open borders with Kruger to the east and Sabi Sands to the west. The game viewing here is reliably superb, with leopards being a particular speciality, and since traversing rights are limited to these camps, good sightings very seldom get oversubscribed.
✛ 229 E4
✉ MalaMala Game Reserve
☎ 011 442 2267
⊕ www.malamala.com

Ngala RRR
This game lodge has 21 thatched cottages decorated with exquisite antiques, sheltered by mopane trees and overlooking a waterhole and large swimming pool. Rates are all-inclusive of game activities and the guides are superb. Suitable for families, though there's one deluxe honeymoon suite.
✛ 229 E4
✉ Timbavati Private Nature Reserve
☎ 011 809 4300
⊕ www.andbeyond.com

Singita Lebombo Lodge RRR
Singita is actually a group of luxury game lodges. Ebony and Boulders lodges are in the Sabi Sands Game Reserve, while

The design of the ultra-luxurious Singita Lebombo Lodge is based on a bird's nest and has impressive open-plan suites and large verandas

Lebombo and Sweni are in a concession-aire part of Kruger near the border with Mozambique. All are design masterpieces using a combination of thatch, wood, glass and steel with bright furnishings and modern art. With fine food and wine, superb game guides and a spa, this is a top safari experience.

✛ 229 E4 (Sabi Sands)
✉ Various, see website for specific lodge details ☎ 021 683 3424
🌐 www.singita.co.za

Skukuza and Lower Sabie R
The largest of Kruger's restcamps, Skukuza overlooks the Sabie River in the game-rich south of the park. Excellent facilities include a restaurant, three swimming pools and a golf course. You can stay in self-catering units or camp. The smaller Lower Sabie camp nearby also lies on the Sabie River.

✛ 229 F4
✉ Near Paul Kruger Gate
☎ 013 735 4265
🌐 www.sanparks.org

PANORAMA ROUTE

Zebra at the Blyde River Canyon Lodge

Blyde River Canyon Lodge RR
This intimate thatched lodge is on the road to the Blyde River Dam at the northern entrance of the canyon. Set in calm, scenic grounds, the nine air-conditioned rooms are modern and comfortable, each with a garden terrace; there's a pool and zebra stroll across the lawns.

✛ 229 E4 ✉ Off the R531, 67km (41mi) from the Orpen Gate
☎ 015 795 5305
🌐 www.blyderivercanyonlodge.com

Hulala Lakeside Lodge RR
This tranquil retreat, which is popular with couples, is wonderfully situated on the shores of Da Gama Lake. The suites all have lake views and a private terrace, there is also a swimming pool and the lodge's traditionally decorated Feathers Restaurant. The complex also includes the Rock Inn Bar. Johannesburg or the Kruger National Park are within a 3–4 hour drive.

✛ 229 E4
✉ Farm Etna R40, 1240 White River
☎ 013 764 1893 🌐 www.hulala.co.za

The Royal Hotel R
When you stay in this 1896 hotel you can imagine what life was like as an early gold prospector in historic Pilgrim's Rest. With original wooden walls and tin roofs, the rooms are in 10 buildings around the village and have been restored with reproduction antiques. There are no TVs but soak up the village's history from the memorabilia in the bar and restaurant.

✛ 229 E3
✉ Main Street, Pilgrim's Rest
☎ 013 768 1100
🌐 www.pilgrims-rest.co.za/stay/royalhotel

MAPUNGUBWE NATIONAL PARK

Leokwe Camp R
The largest camp in Mapungubwe National Park lies in the eastern section, in a valley surrounded by spectacular sandstone hills, a 15-minute drive from the main entrance gate. All units are self-catering. Facilities include a shared swimming pool and picnic area, as well as a nearby treetop hide for birdwatching.

✛ 229 D5
✉ 10km (6mi) north of main entrance gate
☎ 015 534 7923
🌐 www.sanparks.org

Where to...
Eat and Drink

Expect to pay for a two-course meal per person excluding drinks:

R	under R200
RR	R200–R350
RRR	over R350

MBOMBELA

Kuzuri Restaurant RR
Set on a wooden deck overlooking the main waterfall in Mbombela's lush botanical garden, this tranquil place serves up a cosmopolitan à la carte menu with a good selection of Cape Malay dishes.
✝ 229 E3
✉ Shop 57, Sonpark Centre, Nelspruit
☎ 013 757 0907
🕐 Tue–Sun 8:30am–10pm, Mon closed

PANORAMA ROUTE

Canimambo Restaurant RR
Spicy chicken *piri-piri*, grilled lemon butter prawns and other excellent seafood dishes are the specialities at this popular restaurant serving Portuguese and Mozambican fare. There are also regular live entainment events.
✝ 229 E3
✉ Corner Louis Trichardt and Hoof streets, Graskop
☎ 013 767 1868
🌐 www.facebook.com/canimambo. restaurant.graskop
🕐 Daily 11–9

Gum Treez Pub & Grill R–RR
This little complex, on the White River side of Casterbridge Centre under some huge gum trees, consists of a coffee shop for breakfasts or teas, a pub and a restaurant. The best place to sit is outside on the covered deck. The atmosphere is laid-back and relaxed and the menu features South African favourites (lots of meat dishes) but also fish and chips, curries and bunny chow (see page 215).
✝ 229 E3
✉ Casterbridge Lifestyle Centre, White River
☎ 013 750 0334
🌐 www.facebook.com/gumtreezpubandgrill
🕐 Mon–Thu 10–9, Fri, Sat 9–9, Sun 9–3

Harrie's Pancakes R
Harrie's, which now has outlets countrywide, is renowned for its pancakes and there is a divine selection of fillings to choose from, including trout mousse, spicy butternut pumpkin, blue-cheese sauce, banana and caramel, and black cherries and liqueur...nice, friendly atmosphere.
✝ 229 E3
✉ Louis Trichardt Street, Graskop
☎ 013 767 1273
🌐 www.harriespancakes.com
🕐 Daily 8–5:30

The Wild Fig Tree RR
There is a wide veranda for alfresco eating at this friendly spot. Grab a coffee or light lunch during the day, or something more ambitious in the evening – crocodile, venison and trout, a local speciality, are all on the menu. The home-made cakes and desserts are legendary and there's a curio shop where you can browse after you've eaten.
✝ 229 E3 ✉ Corner Main Road and Louis Trichardt Street, Sabie
☎ 013 764 2239
🌐 http://thewildfig.co.za
🕐 Mon–Sat noon–10:30, Sun noon–9

The Windmill Wine Shop R
Within the country's most northerly vineyard, this is a wine shop and deli with a selection of tables as well so you can stop off on your journey and dine. Make up your own platter of tapas, cheese, sliced meat, pickles and olives accompanied by freshly made, still-warm bread, all stacked on rustic wooden boards. Wine is available by the glass and locally brewed beer is on tap.
✝ 229 E3
✉ R536 between Hazyview and Sabie
☎ 082 930 6289
🌐 www.thewindmill.co.za
🕐 Mon–Sat 9–5

HOEDSPRUIT

The Hat & Creek RR
Although this restaurant is large and often busy, the staff are dedicated and attentive. The menu features traditional South African meat dishes – from the perfect steak to the classic burger – along with some seafood and vegetarian dishes. The food is excellent, the portions generous and the atmosphere pleasant and relaxed.

✛ 229 E4
✉ R527, Main Street, Hoedspruit
☎ 015 793 1135
🕐 Daily 9am–10pm

Mad Dogz Café R
A worthwhile stop en route to Kruger's Orpen Gate and the private reserves, this delightful country café, with its shady terrace under thatch, serves up South African favourites such as *bobotie* (a type of shepherd's pie with a savoury custard topping), chicken livers, smoked trout and Cajun dishes. Try one of their burgers and the delicious mango smoothie. The farm breakfasts are a great way to start the day. The service is friendly and accommodating and the attached Monsoon Gallery is worth a browse.

✛ 229 E4
✉ R527, 28km (17mi) from Hoedspruit at the bottom of Blyde River Canyon
☎ 084 250 1233
🌐 www.bluecottages.co.za
🕐 Daily 7:30–4:30

MAGOEBASKLOOF PASS

The Iron Crown Pub and Bistro R
Set amid the pretty Magoebaskloof Mountains, this country pub with a long wooden bar attracts families for Sunday lunch. It is popular for its meaty fare, such as juicy burgers, prime steaks, ribs and chicken schnitzel, accompanied by a variety of sauces. Service is friendly and informal and there are big-screen TVs for important matches – don't expect a quiet drink.

✛ 229 D4
✉ Haenertsburg village on the R71
☎ 015 276 4755
🌐 www.facebook.com/theironcrown
🕐 Tue–Sat 11–late, Sun 9–4

Harrie's Pancakes in Graskop is renowned for its delicious selection of savoury and sweet treats

Where to...Shop

MBOMBELA

An abundance of citrus and other subtropical fruits, including mangoes, bananas, pawpaws and guavas, are grown in this region, as well as nuts. Buy these from the roadside or stop at one of the many country farm stalls (known as *padstal* in Afrikaans).

The provincial capital Mbombela has one of Mpumalanga's largest shopping malls, the Riverside Mall, (tel: 013 757 0080; www.riversidemall.co.za, Mon–Sat 9–6, Sun 9–3), which is 5km (3mi) out of town on the White River road; it has 140 shops, 15 restaurants, a cinema and casino. It's worth stopping here to stock up on food in the supermarkets if you're heading to self-catering accommodation in Kruger.'

The Kruger Lowveld Tourist Information (tel: 013 755 1988) office is located in the Crossing Shopping Centre in Mbombela. Casterbridge Lifestyle Centre (tel: 013 751 1540; www.casterbridge.co.za, Mon–Sat 9–4:30, Sun 9–4), 2km (1mi) beyond White River on the R40, is an attractive country shopping centre where there are also several restaurants and a cinema. Shops sell second-hand books, art, home-made food, jewellery and clothes. This is also where you will also find a small 30-room boutique hotel and a fitness centre and spa.

In Casterbridge, Rottcher Wineries (tel: 013 751 3472) sells Avalencia, a wine-like drink made from fermented orange juice and cane sugar. It is produced on a working macadamia nut farm and the shop at Casterbridge sells nuts as well as orange and ginger liquors in stone jugs.

Across the road from the Casterbridge Farm, the Bagdad Centre is a small centre with shops selling African handicrafts and a delicatessen selling fresh trout, cheeses and jam.

PANORAMA ROUTE

Sabie and Graskop have plenty of curio shops and numerous roadside stalls aimed at tourists, and African carvings markets can be found in the car parks at the viewpoints at some of the waterfalls and Blyde River Canyon.

In Sabie, there's an excellent book shop called The Bookcase (Woodsman Centre, Main Street; tel: 013 764 2014, Mon–Sat 8:30–5, Sun 8:30–3), which is stuffed full of new

The historic cottages lining the street in Pilgrim's Rest appear frozen in time

HOEDSPRUIT

On the R527 at the bottom of Blyde River Canyon, towards Hoedspruit, are a couple of places worth venturing to, including Monsoon Gallery (R527, east of the junction with the R36; tel: 015 795 5114; http://bluecottages. co.za/monsoon-gallery), which sells a wonderful selection of quality ethnic jewellery, pottery, rural art, embroidery, baskets and wildlife books. Some of the items are antique and the owner is an avid collector of tribal artefacts. It's next to the Mad Dogz Café.

Nearby is Godding & Godding on the 24 Degrees South farm (on the R531; tel: 072 467 3310; www.goddingandgodding. com), 20km (12mi) south of Hoedspruit, which among other items makes divinely luxurious silk duvets. You can go on a tour to learn how silk is made and about the lifecycle of a silkworm.

Where to...Go out

As you're in the countryside, there is naturally little in the way of nightlife. But there are plenty of outdoor activities in the area to entertain you.

The Big Swing (Panorama Gorge, on the R533 a few metres outside of Graskop towards Hazyview; tel: 079 779 8713; www. bigswing.co.za) is similar to a bungee jump but with more of an outward swing over the pretty Panorama Falls.

The region's rivers are ideal for whitewater rafting day trips and overnight trips can be arranged through a number of operators via Sabie River Adventures (tel: 013 492 0071; http://sabieriveradventures.co.za).

The Blyde River Canyon looks even more impressive from the air (Sunrise Aviation; tel: 083 625 6991; www.sunrisehelicopters. co.za), or take an early morning balloon ride (Suncatchers; tel: 087 806 2097; www.sun-catchers.co.za).

At Shangana Cultural Village 5km (3mi) from Hazyview on the R535 towards Graskop (tel: 013 737 5804; www.shangana.co.za) there are daily tours of the authentic village, although the best time to go is for the evening festival.

Dancer in the Shangana Cultural Village

and used books including a very good section on South African history.

In Hazyview, Perry's Bridge Trading Post (Main Street; tel: 013 737 6929; www. perrysbridge.co.za, Mon–Fri 7:30–4) has a number of interesting shops including a deli, a shop selling imported chocolates, a tourist information office, a reptile park (www.perrysbridgereptilepark.com) and several restaurants.

The Marula Market (five minutes from Hazyview on the R535 toward Graskop; tel: 013 737 5804; www.shangana.co.za) at Shangana Cultural Village is a wide circle of huts surrounded by trees and is home to craftspeople from all over the region; it has been an important catalyst for enabling local artists to make a living.

The long single street in Pilgrim's Rest is lined with gift and curio shops as well as restaurants, many of them housed in restored miners' cottages.

Thunderclouds over the Kalahari Desert in the
Kgalagadi Transfrontier National Park

Northwest & Central Regions

A region of hidden treasures, from diamonds to the flower seeds lying dormant under the desert sands.

Getting Your Bearings

Few visitors venture to the northern reaches
of the country. It can be hot in places,
there are long distances to cover, and towns
and settlements are few and far between.
However, the area will appeal to the adventurer
and there are some wonderful experiences
to be had in its remote regions.

Boundless semi-desert plains and sculptural, craggy mountains characterise the Northern Cape. The secrets of the desert are its true treasures: succulents than store water in their stems and roots, seeds that explode into improbable carpets of flowers after a spattering of rain, and diamonds in the vents of its subterranean volcanoes.

The Kalahari section is home to the San and the Nama, the last nomadic peoples of southern Africa, and despite the arid landscape, offers a diverse wildlife habitat. The largest wilderness is in Botswana and Namibia, on the border with South Africa, an area that forms the magnificent Kgalagadi Transfrontier Park.

Not far from Johannesburg is the gambler's playground of Sun City, a world away from the adjoining wildlife sanctuaries of Pilanesberg and Madikwe. Inland is the Free State Province, dominated by endless wheat fields, while the mountains of the Eastern Highlands rise scenically on the eastern border to Lesotho.

TOP 10
⑤ ★★ Pilanesberg National Park

Don't Miss
㊺ Sun City
㊻ Madikwe Game Reserve
㊼ Kgalagadi Transfrontier Park

At Your Leisure
48 Eastern Highlands
49 Bloemfontein
50 Kimberley
51 Upington
52 Augrabies Falls National Park

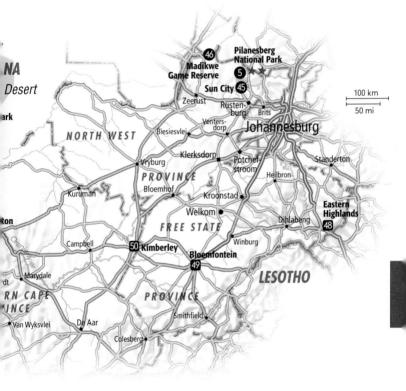

NA

Desert

ark

NORTH WEST

PROVINCE

46 Madikwe
Game Reserve

5 Pilanesberg
National Park

Sun City **45**

Zeerust

Rustenburg

Brits

Venters-dorp

Johannesburg

Biesiesvlei

Klerksdorp

Vryburg

Potchef-stroom

Standerton

Kuruman

Bloemhof

Heilbron

Kroonstad

Welkom

FREE STATE

Dihlabeng

**Eastern
Highlands** **48**

Campbell

50 Kimberley

Winburg

Bloemfontein
49

Marydale

LESOTHO

dt

RN CAPE

NCE

PROVINCE

Van Wyksvlei

De Aar

Smithfield

Colesberg

100 km

50 mi

ton

My Day
in the Grip
of Diamond Fever

South Africa ranks seventh among the world's diamond producers and the Big Hole in Kimberley is where its success story began. Spend a day following the glittering trail of these gems with your starting point being the Big Hole Centre (www.thebighole.co.za).

10am: How it all Began

Start the guided tour at the Big Hole. The world's second largest hand-dug hole is 215m (705ft) deep and has a perimeter of 1.6km (1mi). Started in the 1870s, the mine yielded three tons of diamonds from its depths. The tour begins with a film detailing the mine's history, then you walk out onto the open-air viewing platform high above the water of the Big Hole.

11am: Background and Underground

Next up you get to experience what it must have been like for the miners who had to descend more than 1,000m (3,300ft) deep underground. A lift takes you down a mineshaft. It actually only goes down a few metres, but the audio effects guarantee a very realistic experience. Afterwards, the exhibits at the Mine Museum explain everything you have ever wanted to know about diamonds.

10am: How it all Began

Roper St

lar Rd

Bar

10am

City Hall

Big Hole

Old Main St

End

Kimberley Club

2:30pm: Mining Magnate Mansions

ircular Rd

Bultfontein

Lennox St

Aristotle Ave

Queens Park

Du Toit Span St

2:30pm

BELGRAVIA

200 m
200 yd

Start

William Humphries Art Gallery

Rudd House

Lodge Rd

Civic Centre

Diamond Vault

Noon

Loch Rd

Dunluce

11am: Background and Underground

Noon: Diamonds Galore...

Big Hole museum complex includes authentic houses and vintage vehicles

Noon: Diamonds Galore...
...is what you will see at the well-guarded <u>diamond vault</u>, which holds 3,500 diamonds as well as a replica of the Eureka. The 21-carat original was found in 1867 and triggered the diamond rush. Now, you have earned a respite so take a ride around the Big Hole on a <u>restored tram</u> (R10).

1pm: High Noon in the Museum Village
The museum town around the Big Hole Centre depicts the Kimberley of the late 19th century. The original buildings (pub, shop, bank etc.) were dismantled in other parts of the country and reconstructed here. This is a pleasant place for a stroll

and for a browse around the souvenir shops. At lunchtime you can pop into the <u>Occidental Bar</u> (16W Circular Road; tel: 053 831 1296) for a burger and a craft beer.

2:30pm: Mining Magnate Mansions
The wealth earned by the Big Hole's mining magnates was proudly put on display in the elegant suburb of <u>Belgravia</u>. On Loch Road you will see numerous mansion such as <u>Rudd House</u> (number 5–7), where Cecil Rhodes' business partner once lived. Kimberley's first mayor and chairman of De Beers Consolidated, Ernest Oppenheimer, lived around the corner in a handsome house on <u>Lodge Road</u> (number 7). The late-Victorian

Centre above: Kimberley's historic City Hall
Centre below: Teatime at the William Humphreys Art Gallery
Right: Tasty seafood in the Rhodes Grill

Dunluce (number 10), which was built in 1897, is especially attractive.

3:30pm: Tea for Two
Time for a break, so head over to the tearoom in the William Humphreys Art Gallery (1 Cullinan Crescent; www.whag.co.za; Mon–Fri 8–4:45, Sat 10–4:45, Sun 9–noon; R5), where you can enjoy tea and cake while enjoying a view of the Oppenheimer Gardens. The historic City Hall on Market Street is the last stop on your walk and then it's time

for a short siesta in your hotel. For your evening dinner you'll need to smarten up for the refined elegance of the Kimberley Club.

7pm: Historic Dining Venue
Order a taxi to take you to the Kimberley Club (72 Du Toitspan Rd; tel: 053 832 4224; www.kimberley club.co.za), which dates back to the late 19th century and retains echoes of its golden era. The Rhodes Grill is decorated with memorabilia and photos from the club's past.

❺ ★★ Pilanesberg National Park

Don't Miss	Wildlife paradise near to Johannesburg
Why	The Big Five along with other aquatic wildlife, such as hippos and crocodiles
Time	One day
When	The best time for game viewing is the dry season (May–Oct)
What Else	A thrilling ride in a hot air balloon
In Short	An abundance of birdlife!

This national park is in the transition area between the dry Kalahari and the humid lowveld. Nestled in the eroded caldera of the long-extinct 1,687m-high (5,535ft) Pilanesberg volcano, the reserve is one of the largest and most popular wildlife sanctuaries in South Africa. In addition to the Big Five there are a wealth of other animals to see, including 300 bird species.

Established in the 1970s, it lies northwest of Johannesburg, adjacent to Sun City, making it a natural haven for weekend getaways. The park was stocked with animals from all over the country in the successful reintroduction project Operation Genesis. Today, it supports an estimated 10,000 large mammals representing about 25 species. It is a particularly good place for spotting white rhino and elephant, but black rhino, lion, leopard and buffalo are also present and seen with some regularity. Common herbivores include giraffe, plains zebra, blue wildebeest, warthog, impala and greater kudu. The park also hosts several antelope species that are absent or rare further east, including the black wildebeest, which are on the Red List of Threatened Species.

Waterhole Rendezvous

Set right in the centre of the park, Mankwe Dam is the habitat of crocodile, hippo and water-associated birds such as the handsome African fish eagle and various herons, storks and kingfishers. A hide overlooks the dam, and there are several other hides scattered at smaller watering points too.

There are numerous lodges and camps within the park, and the main entrance gate is less than 5km (3mi) from Sun City. A thrilling way to see the landscape of the Pilanesberg National Park is to go game viewing in a hot air balloon. The views and animals are fantastic and the whole adventure takes about 5 hours (60 minutes of which is pure flight time).

A herd of black wildebeest grazing in the park's open savannah

INSIDER TIP The park has five picnic areas, the most attractive of which is **Fish Eagle**, which overlooks Mankwe Dam. There's also a quiet **coffee shop** at the Pilanesberg Centre in a converted old farmhouse north of Mankwe Dam.

✚ 228 B3
✉ Off the R565 ☎ 014 555 1600
🌐 www.northwestparks.org.za
🕐 Nov–Feb daily 5:30–7; Mar, Apr, Sep, Oct 6–6:30; May–Aug 6:30–6 💰 R110

**Hot Air Balloon Safari/
Mankwe Game Trackers**
☎ 014 552 5020
🌐 www.mankwegametrackers.co.za
💰 R4,750

45 Sun City

Don't Miss	Take a break from game viewing
Why	Glitzy hotels, a massive casino, water adventure park, golf courses and live shows
Time	One to two days
When	Day and night
What Else	Man-made beaches entirely free of sharks!
In Short	South Africans having fun

Tucked away in the lush rolling bush of the former homeland of Bophuthatswana is the Las Vegas of South Africa, a huge, brash entertainment resort that attracts 25,000 guests daily.

Gambling was illegal in South Africa during the apartheid era but as it was legal in the black homelands, this was where the casino resorts were built. This explains the rather remote location of Sun City, which was built in 1979 in the former homeland of Bophuthatswana. Today, there's less emphasis on gambling at Sun City (one casino remains open) and the complex is more geared to family entertainment. You can

stay overnight or visit on a long day trip from Johannesburg or Pretoria. You'll not be short of things to do here; the whole complex can be explored from the Sky Train monorail that starts in the parking area, and you can pick up a map, and pre-book activities in the resort's Welcome Centre. The resort's extravagant recreational facilities include one of the world's largest casinos, numerous cinemas, nightclubs, a huge range of water sports and two golf courses. The arena hosts sporting events and pop concerts.

Sun City is Africa's answer to Las Vegas – pictured here is the luxurious Palace of the Lost City hotel

Lost City Living

The complex is dominated by <u>The Lost City,</u> which symbolises a legend in African culture, one that actually never existed. In the centre of the Lost City is <u>The Palace of the Lost City</u> a luxury hotel with a 25m-high (82ft) lobby that feels more like a cathedral. All accommodation at the Palace of the Lost City, Sun City Hotel, Cascades and the Sun City Cabanas must be booked through Sun International Central Reservations (tel: 011 780 7800; www.suninternational.com).

All Artificial?

Below the hotel is the Valley of the Waves, a man-made 25ha (62-acre) tropical rainforest with water park. The Roaring Lagoon, a pool area created using shipped in beach sand, has waves that are mechanically generated so that water surges up the beach. To create an "authentic" African experience, animal sounds are played on loudspeakers.

Visitors to Sun City's Valley of the Waves enjoying the man-made beaches and wave pool

INSIDER TIP At the **Cultural Village** there's a *shebeen* (pub) that serves African cuisine, and you can also watch traditional singing and dancing.

✚ 228 B3 ✉ On the R565 north of Rustenburg ☎ 014 557 1000

🌐 www.suninternational.com
💰 R75, Valley of the Waves R160–R190

㊻ Madikwe Game Reserve

Don't Miss	Impressive wildlife in a malaria-free region
Why	The Big Five and very professional guides
Time	One or two days
When	Best in the dry season of May–October
What Else	Opulent and exclusive lodges
In Short	Superlative South Africa!

A male southern masked weaver (*Ploceus velatus*) building a nest

This 750km² (290mi²) reserve was established in 1991 and lies in the far north of the country, on the border with Botswana. As the reserve is compact, game viewing here is often more successful than in the better-known Kruger National Park.

Scenically, the reserve consists of vast plains of open woodland and grasslands, a landscape that tends to be rather uniform in the east, but is dotted with rocky hills in the west, while the Dwarsberg Mountains lie close to the southern boundary. The most important river is the Marico, which flows along the eastern boundary. Closed to day visitors and self-drive safaris, Madikwe is serviced by about 16 luxury lodges and guests explore the reserve in guided game drives. The all-inclusive (accommodation, meals and game drives) safari packages are not cheap, but worth the expense as the animals have become accustomed to the open game drive vehicles and don't see the game rangers – and their guests – as a threat. So your ranger may switch off the vehicle in the middle of a buffalo herd and not even the clicking of cameras will disturb the herd as they graze. The rangers also communicate with each other via radio, so if one finds a family of lions resting under an acacia tree, they will let the other guides know.

The reserve was primarily established to protect endangered animals but it has also created jobs for the local population.

Operation Phoenix

Similar to Operation Genesis (the Pilanesberg reintroduction project), Madikwe's <u>Operation Phoenix</u> ran from 1991 to 1998 when 28 different mammal species, and a total of 8,000 animals, were resettled here from other South African game reserves. All the animals, including elephant herds, were originally native to the region, but were almost completely wiped out by hunting and farming.

Diversity Between Bushveld and Desert

In addition to the Big Five, the reserve's open grassland is also one of the best places anywhere to see the endangered African wild dog. More than 350 varieties of bird have been recorded in the reserve, ranging from ostrich and kori bustard (the world's heaviest flying bird) to the pied babbler and violet-eared waxbill, and an impressive selection of eagles and other raptors.

Antelope and zebra near Jaci's Lodge, one of the 16 luxury lodges in Madikwe

INSIDER TIP Enjoy lavish brunches and afternoon tea in the **luxury lodges** before and after game drives.

✛ 228 B4
✉ Off the R49 north of Zeerust
No day visitors to the reserve

☎ 018 350 9931/2
🌐 www.northwestparks.org.za
🍃 R180, in addition to accommodation

47 Kgalagadi Transfrontier Park

Don't Miss	Captivating desert wilderness
Why	Crimson sand dunes and desert-adapted wildlife
Time	One or two days
When	In the cooler months (May–September) to avoid the unbearable heat
What Else	Cute and entertaining meerkats
In Short	Unforgettable night sky studded with stars

Expect red sand dunes that extend to the horizon, camelthorn trees in river valleys, herds of gemsbok, majestic giraffes, prides of lazy Kalahari lions and at night you'll hear the sound of the hyenas giggling – the Kgalagadi (a Tswana name) offers a fascinating, unspoilt desert landscape that is a wonderful contrast to the rest of the country's national parks.

As a cross-border protected area the Kgalagadi Transfrontier Park is one of the so-called Peace Parks

The arid Kalahari basin stretches over a more than 1 million km² (385,000mi²), the largest area is in Botswana, the western region is in Namibia and only the southern tip is in South Africa. The vast 38,000km² (14,700mi²) cross-border Kgalagadi Transfrontier Park was created by the merger of Botswana's Gemsbok National Park and South Africa's Kalahari Gemsbok National Park. Two usually dry rivers, the Auob and the Nossob, cross the park from northwest to southeast and form the main arteries along which game drives take place.

Blazing Orange Sundowner

When you leave for your late afternoon game
drive in the Kgalagadi Transfrontier Park,
take along a cooler box with a bottle of chilled
white wine and two glasses. Then, just before
the sun goes down, park at the foot of a sand
dune, climb up to the ridge and open your
wine. Watch as the sky turns royal blue, the
dunes glow orange, the shadows grow longer
and the gemsbok stroll past below you...
a sundowner during the most magical minutes
of the day.

Top left: Kalahari lions can go without water for up to two weeks. Top right: A well-camouflaged, sand-coloured ground squirrel. Left: Gemsbok is a variety of antelope common in the park

Man and Nature in the Kalahari

The vast arid plains are covered by a layer of red, iron oxide sand, formed by the erosion of huge rock masses. The luminous, multi-shaded dune landscapes alternate with expanses of dry savannah.

Due to its inhospitable conditions, the Kalahari is a virtually untouched wilderness; only the San roam its endless expanses.

It is a thirst land – as opposed to a waterless desert devoid of any life – and the part within South Africa receives an average rainfall of 200mm (8in) per annum, which allows for some vegetation. Plants that are well adapted to the dry conditions include dwarf shrubs, grass tussocks and succulents. One of the few tree species is the white-barked shepherd tree, which has a shady canopy of evergreen leaves. Beautiful camelthorn trees, which grow in dry river valleys, can grow up to 15m (50ft). After rain showers the desert landscape is briefly transformed by an array of grasses and flowers. Although there are two riverbeds (the Auob and the Nossob) running through the park, they have only flowed a few times in the last century. Over millennia flash floods have nonetheless caused the rivers to carve out impressive valleys. About 80 windmills along the river valleys provide water for the park's animals. Another source of water is the Tsamma, a wild melon that is 90 per cent water.

The Desert is Alive

In addition to the gemsbok, found here in numbers, there are also numerous blue wildebeest, eland and hartebeest. Among the 200 varieties of birds are 50 raptors. Game viewing is at its best in the dry valleys and around the waterholes.

There are 10 camps on the South African side. The largest is Twee Rivieren, which lies at the entrance gate, and is fenced with a shop, restaurant, swimming pool and petrol station. Mata-Mata and Nossob are also relatively large fenced camps with similar facilities. !Xaus Lodge is an isolated community-owned upmarket tented camp overlooking a saltpan; the lodge also offers guided nature walks.

INSIDER TIP About 50km (30mi) before the park's gate is the **Kgalagadi Lodge** (tel: 054 325 0935; www.kgalagadi-lodge. co.za; R) the last stop before the park. There's a restaurant, a supermarket, a bakery and a butcher.

---

227 D4
385km (239mi) from Kuruman, 260km (161mi) from Upington
054 561 2000

www.sanparks.org
Twee Rivieren gate hours vary every month but are generally open 7–6:30 R328

At Your Leisure

48 Eastern Highlands

In the middle of the country, the Free State Province is dominated by an undulating grassy plain with fields of corn and sunflowers. In the southeast, however, it abruptly rises to a highland area bordering Lesotho, where the Golden Gate Highlands National Park derives its name from the brilliant shades of gold cast by the sun on the park's sandstone cliffs. The grasslands and hills offer superb hiking and birdwatching, and there's a hotel and a restcamp. Just before the park's western gate, the Basotho Cultural Village gives insights into the lives of the Basotho people. You can tour the village huts, watch craft workers and sample the home-made beer.

Further west, the village of Clarens is an artists' refuge thanks to the pretty mountain scenery, and you can visit a number of galleries situated around the village square.

✈ 229 D1
Golden Gate Highlands National Park
☎ 058 255 1000
🌐 www.sanparks.org 🏷 R192
Basotho Cultural Village
🕐 Daily 9–4
🏷 Guided tour R70
Clarens Tourist Information
✉ Market Street, Clarens
☎ 058 256 1542 🌐 www.clarens.co.za
🕐 Daily 9–1, 2–5

The diamond deposits found in and around Kimberley are not alluvial but embedded in volcanic kimberlite rock – pictured here is the Big Hole where diamonds were excavated up until 1914

49 Bloemfontein

Straddling the N1 highway, Bloemfontein, the capital of the Free State Province and part of the Mangaung Metropolitan Municipality, is a convenient overnight stop for motorists going between Johannesburg and Cape Town and there are scores of accommodation options. The city centre is home to some historical, tree-lined streets concentrated around President Brand Street, with some stately government buildings like the City Hall, the Old Presidency, the Anglican Cathedral, the twin-tower Dutch Reformed Church and the Supreme Court. The tourist office offers a map of a historical walking tour. The National Museum has displays on dinosaurs and natural history as well as a mock-up of an early street in Bloemfontein. To the northeast of the city centre is Naval Hill, which is worth driving up for the broad city views, and at the top is the Franklin Game Reserve, which is home to some springbok, eland and hartebeest and giraffe. Bloemfontein is where the author J RR Tolkien, creator of *The Hobbit* and *Lord of the Rings*, was born.

+ 228 B1 ✉ 60 Park Road ☎ 051 405 8489
⊕ www.bloemfontein.co.za,
www.mangaung.co.za
🕐 Mon–Fri 8–4:30, Sat 8–noon
National Museum
✉ 36 Aliwal Street ☎ 051 447 9609
⊕ www.nasmus.co.za 🕐 Mon–Fri 8–5,
Sat 10–5, Sun noon–5 🐾 R5

50 Kimberley

Kimberley, the capital of the Northern Cape, is synonymous with diamonds. These were discovered here in 1871, attracting a rush of prospectors who collectively excavated the Big Hole, mining some 14.5 million carats before the Hole's closure in 1914. At the time, at 460m (1,500ft) wide (1.6km/1mi perimeter) and 240m (790ft) deep, it was the world's largest hand-dug hole. Today, the Big Hole Complex includes a museum dedicated to the diamond rush, when prospectors lit their cigars with banknotes and bathed in Champagne, and more millionaires – among them Cecil John Rhodes – met at the Kimberley Club than anywhere else in the world.

+ 228 A1
The Big Hole Complex
✉ Tucker Street
☎ 053 839 4600
⊕ www.thebighole.co.za
🕐 Daily 8–5 🐾 R110

51 Upington

Upington is the most substantial town for hundreds of kilometres in any direction and the main gateway to the Kgalagadi Transfrontier Park (p.176), so you'll no doubt end up here if you tour the remote northwest. Here the Gariep River (formerly the Orange River) irrigates a narrow ribbon of fertile land where wine grapes are cultivated, and sultanas and raisins produced. Upington is home to the Orange River Wine Cellars Co-operative and the South African Dried Fruit Co-operative, so look out for these items for sale. The town developed from a mission station, founded in 1871, and the history can be seen in the little <u>Kalahari Oranje Museum</u>, which has the town's best view of the river. Upington is the country's hottest town; summer temperatures often rise to more than 40°C (104°F).

Augrabies Falls is a "place of great noise"

✠ 227 D2
Upington Information Centre
✉ Mutual Street
☎ 054 338 71 51
⊕ www.zfm-dm.co.za
● Mon–Fri 8–5:30, Sat 9–noon
Kalahari Oranje Museum
✉ 4 Short Street
● Mon–Fri 9–12:30, 2–5
✈ R30

52 Augrabies Falls National Park
The Augrabies Falls are where the Gariep (Orange) River drops 100m (328ft) over a series of cataracts before thundering down through a small rocky gap in an explosion of white water into the 18km (11mi) Orange River Gorge. For good reason the Khoi people called it Aukoerebis, meaning "place of great noise". The best time to see the falls is in late summer when the river carries a lot of water and additional waterfalls form on the side walls of the gorge and the air is full of spray. Surrounding the gorge is a lunar-like landscape of eroded rock, and the rest of the park is semi-desert and home to a number of small mammals and some reintroduced black rhino. The most characteristic plant in the park is the giant aloe called *kokerboom* (quiver tree), which gets its name from the Bushmen (San) who use the soft branches to make quivers for their arrows. The Augrabies Restcamp, managed by South African National Parks (SANParks), has a good range of simple self-catering accommodation and a campsite with swimming pools, and there's a restaurant and bar. Reservations for night drives can be made at reception.

✠ 226 C2
✉ 120km (74mi) west of Upington
☎ 054 452 9200
⊕ www.sanparks.org
● Daily 7:30–6:30 ✈ R192

Where to...Stay

Expect to pay in high season per double room per night

R   under R1,500
RR   R1,500–R3,000
RRR over R3,000

Bakubung Bush Lodge R
Bakubung Bush Lodge is quite large; it offers both hotel rooms as well as about 60 self-catering chalets. All have views of a waterhole and the undulating Pilanesberg hills. The lodge's elegant Marula Grill Restaurant serves a buffet as well as tempting grilled meat, seafood and pasta dishes.
✈ 228 B3 ✉ Pilanesberg National Park, Kubu Street, Rustenburg
☎ 014 552 6000 ⊕ www.legacyhotels.co.za/hotels/bakubung-bush-lodge

Hobbit Boutique Hotel R
The furnishings and setting of this hotel will make you feel a bit like Bilbo in the Shire. All of the rooms are named after characters from the *Lord of the Rings* trilogy and are adorned with pictures and maps painted by Tolkien.
✈ 228 B1 ✉ 19 President Steyn Avenue, Westdene, Bloemfontein
☎ 051 447 0663
⊕ www.hobbit.co.za

Kimberley Country House RR
Conveniently located in the middle of town, close to all the attractions, this 10-bedroom guest house offers Victorian era charm with modern amenities (WiFi, air conditioning). The team of staff are friendly and helpful, the breakfast is excellent and when it gets too hot you can cool off in the swimming pool.
✈ 228 A1 ✉ 6 Carrington Road, Belgravia, Kimberley
☎ 076 388 0756
⊕ www.kchouse.co.za

Kwa Maritane/Tshukudu RRR
Kwa Maritane is in the southeast of Pilanesberg National Park, right next to an entrance gate, with a hide overlooking a busy waterhole, yet only a 10-minute drive from Sun City. Under the same management, the more exclusive Tshukudu lies deep within the park, perched on a rocky outcrop offering superb views over the plains. There are just eight thatched chalets here, and rates include game drives. Both lodges have a swimming pool.
✈ 228 B4
✉ Pilanesberg Game Reserve
☎ 011 806 6888
⊕ www.legacygroup.co.za

Makanyane Safari Lodge RRR
Set on private land on the eastern border of Madikwe Game Reserve, this stunning lodge consists of eight large suites overlooking the Marico River. Top-notch guides lead the game drives and the reliably good wildlife sightings are complemented by fine cuisine and a good wine list. Facilities include a swimming pool, spa and gym.
✈ 228 B4
✉ Access via Makanyane Gate on the dirt road between Sun City and Derdepoort
☎ 014 778 9600
⊕ www.sanctuaryretreats.com

Le Must River Residence and Three Gables Guest House R–RR
Le Must River Residence is a 5-star guest house in the theme of an Italian-style villa with 11 individual rooms overlooking a pool and the river. Three Gables is a very comfortable 3-star guest house with 6 rooms with contemporary African art.
✈ 227 D2 ✉ 14 Butler Street and 12 Murray Avenue, Upington ☎ 054 332 3971
⊕ www.lemustupington.com

Twee Rivieren R
This is Kgalagadi's administrative headquarters and largest restcamp, and is at the entrance of the park. It's also the only camp that has mobile phone reception and 24-hour electricity. There's a pool (essential in this region), campsite, restaurant and petrol station. The air-conditioned cottages are equipped for self-catering groups of up to six.
✈ 227 D4
✉ Kgalagadi Transfrontier Park
☎ 021 428 9111 ⊕ www.sanparks.org

Where to...Eat and Drink

Expect to pay for a two-course meal per person excluding drinks:

R   under R200
RR   R200–R350
RRR over R350

Café Zest R
This casual, tastefully decorated restaurant has a café in the front, an attractive courtyard and a dining area at the rear section. The menu features locally sourced meaty fare, such as whole Kalahari lamb shank but also includes fish, chicken and pasta dishes. There's also a good selection of wines.
✣ 227 D2
✉ 49 Schröder Street, Upington
☎ 054 332 1413
🌐 www.facebook.com/cafezestupington
🕐 Mon–Sat 9am–10pm

Clementine's RR
Don't be put off by the corrugated iron exterior because inside this popular restaurant, close to Clarens's central square, is a well-stocked bar, neat candlelit tables and an affordable menu. Opt for steak with a delicious sauce or grilled fish, followed by imaginative desserts such as chocolate crème brûlée or butternut cheesecake. There's a patio overlooking the mountains.
✣ 224 C5
✉ Church Street, Clarens
☎ 058 256 1616
🌐 www.clementines.co.za
🕐 Tue–Sun 11–3, 6–10

The Occidental Bar (The Ox) RR
This saloon bar in the Big Hole Complex is headed up by Chef Daniel Williams who is well known beyond the borders of Kimberley. Together with his crew he prepares top-quality South African pub food including steaks, chicken, venison, prawns, gourmet burgers and sandwiches. The diamond rush era atmosphere makes it a very nice place to spend an evening, and in the summer, there is an outside area with long tables and benches.
✣ 228 A2 ✉
Big Hole Complex, Tucker Street, Kimberley
☎ 053 831 1296
🕐 Mon–Thu 10–10, Fri, Sat 10–midnight, Sun 12:30–3

De Oude Kraal Country Estate RRR
Locals travel a long way to get to this delightful farmhouse, especially for the Sunday lunch and six-course gourmet evening meals. Surrounded by vines and blue gum trees the restaurant has high ceilings, wooden floors and there's a veranda for alfresco dining. Food is beautifully presented and the wine cellar has some rare vintages. Accommodation is also available and overnight guests can tour the cellar to pick their own wine for dinner.
✣ 228 A1
✉ 35km (22mi) south of Bloemfontein, take the Riversford exit off the N1
☎ 051 564 0733 🌐 www.deoudekraal.com
🕐 Daily 7:30am–9:30pm

Seven on Kellner RR–RRR
This award-winning restaurant, set in a historic mansion in Bloemfontein, has a globetrotting menu with something for everybody, ranging from spicy Moroccan stew to tasty pizzas cooked in a wood-fired oven.
✣ 228 B1
✉ 7 Kellner Street, Bloemfontein
☎ 051 447 7928
🌐 www.sevenonkellner.co.za
🕐 Mon–Thu noon–2, 5–10, Fri, Sat 1–11

Steak Out Grills R
This bustling restaurant, which is located in a shopping mall, has a menu that caters to all (small selection of seafood dishes) but it is the large portions of meat that attracts most of the guests. The draw cards include the Hunter's Steak (with chicken liver and *piri-piri* sauce) and the oversized (almost 1kg) pork knuckle. The selection of food is good, there's a Sunday buffet and carvery, and the service is very friendly and attentive.
✣ 228 B3
✉ Waterfall Mall Shopping Centre, 1 Augrabies Ave, Rustenburg
☎ 014 592 0766 🕐 Daily 8am–10pm

Golf course in Sun City

Where to...Shop

Given that this is a region of wide open spaces, it's not known for shopping. However, you should be able to pick up curios at shops in lodges, and the small towns have supermarkets and bottle stores to top up provisions.

Sun City has a shopping mall and shops in the entertainment complex, Sun Central (tel: 014 557 1000) and its hotels have excellent amenities.

The village of Clarens in the Eastern Highlands has galleries and craft shops gathered around the village square.

The Windmill Centre (365 Main Street, Clarens) has a shop selling home-made body products and sandstone gifts plus cafés while the Johan Smith Gallery (tel: 083 262 3169; www.johansmith.co.za), which specializes in paintings and ceramics, also has a café.

The Clarens Meander Centre (Corner Main/van Zyl streets; tel: 72 601 1576) is a small shopping mall on the approach to the village.

The two premier shopping malls in Bloemfontein are the Mimosa Mall (corner of Nelson Mandela and Parfitt streets; tel: 051 444 6914; www.mimosamall.com), and Loch Logan Waterfront (Henry Street; tel: 051 448 3607; www.lochlogan.co.za), an outdoor mall arranged around a boardwalk overlooking a lake in King's Park.

Kimberley's major shopping mall is Diamond Pavilion (Bloemfontein Rd; tel: 053 832 9200; www.diamondpavilion.co.za).

Upington is the last stop for travellers going to the Kgalagadi Transfrontier Park so take advantage of the supermarkets and stock up on drinks and food.

Where to...Go Out

Nightlife is restricted to dinner in a *boma* (African enclosure), a glass of wine in a hotel bar, or a beer while you barbecue your meat on the grill outside your chalet. There are, however, a number of outdoor pursuits.

SPORT

Sun City (tel: 014 557 1000; www.suninternational.com) is a premier destination for golfers, with two 18-hole, par 72 courses.

In the Eastern Highlands near Clarens, Outrageous Adventures (tel: 083 485 9654; www.outrageousadventures.co.za, Oct–Mar) organizes whitewater rafting day trips on the Ash River with an optional 35m (115ft) abseil down a nearby cliff.

Umkulu Safari and Canoe Trails offer multi-day rafting trips on the Gariep (Orange) River. An adventurous way of seeing the area's wild animals and unique landscape, and you can opt to sleep under the stars or in a tent before returning by bus (tel: 082 082 6715; http://umkuluadventures.com).

FESTIVALS

The 10-day Macufe Festival (www.macufe.co.za) is held in Bloemfontein in early October. One of the biggest festivals in the country, it celebrates African arts and culture.

Connoisseurs of the amber nectar should head to Clarens in February for the Craft Beer Festival (www.clarenscraftbeerfest.com), which showcases the country's top artisanal breweries.

Driving along the Table Mountain National Park coastal road with the Twelve Apostles in the background

Walks & Tours

Out and about in a country that boasts unique nature, flora and fauna, and fascinating ethnicities and cultures.

Pages 186–201

Cape Town City

What	Walk
Distance	Approximately 1.5km (1mi)
Time	1.5 hours
Start/End	Cape Town Tourism, corner of Castle and Burg streets ✛ 232 B2

This short walk in Cape Town's centre will take you through lively streets and busy shopping thoroughfares lined with both impressive historic buildings and modern high-rises.

1–2

From the <u>tourist office</u> walk along Strand Street to the Golden Acre shopping complex and turn right on to Adderley Street. On the left is the fragrant and colourful <u>flower market</u> in Trafalgar Place and next door is the Standard Bank, a good example of late 19th-century architecture. Further up on the other side of the road is the First National Bank designed in 1933 by architect Sir Herbert Baker. Opposite and on the corner of Adderley and Wale streets is the <u>Slave Lodge</u>, built in 1679 as accommodation for slaves.

2–3

Opposite the Slave Lodge is the Anglican <u>St George's Cathedral</u> where Archbishop Desmond Tutu, who received the Nobel Peace Prize in 1984, gave many of his anti-apartheid sermons.

3–4

Next to the cathedral is the start of Government Avenue, where you can stroll among the oak trees, lawns and hedges known as Company's Garden after the Dutch East India Company who first settled in the Cape in the 17th century. In the garden are a number of museums, the National Library of South Africa – which opened in 1818 – and the Houses of Parliament, built in 1884 with a statue of Queen Victoria out front. De Tuynhuys (Afrikaans for "the garden house") is the Cape Town office of the president.

The Houses of Parliament, the seat of the National Assembly

4–5

Return to the cathedral and go left into Wale Street, then turn right into St George's Mall, a pedestrian precinct, and then left along Longmarket Street to Greenmarket Square, the oldest square in the city. Continue along Longmarket and cross Long Street.

6–7

Another block takes you to Loop Street, where on the right-hand corner you'll find Heritage Square, a lovingly restored block of 18th- to 19th-century town houses with bars, restaurants and the Cape Heritage Hotel clustered around a courtyard, which is home to an old vine planted in 1781. Walk north along Loop Street for two blocks, crossing Castle Street and turn right on to Strand Street. Cross Long Street again and on your right is the Koopmans-De Wet House museum. Turn right on to Burg Street and you're back at the tourist office.

INSIDER TIP The **Macau Asian Tavern** serves tasty Asian and Portuguese inspired dishes in a stylish dining section and bar, upstairs is a cocktail lounge (101 Hout Street; tel: 021 422 2400; daily noon–4:00, 6–10:30, RR).

Cape Peninsula

What	Drive
Distance	Approximately 180km (112mi)
Time	1 day
Start/End	Central Cape Town ✈ 230 B2

The ruggedly beautiful Cape Peninsula is dominated by the Table Mountain massif. On both sides of the spine are pretty fishing villages, clutches of luxurious houses, winding roads that hug the cliffs and ever-present ocean views.

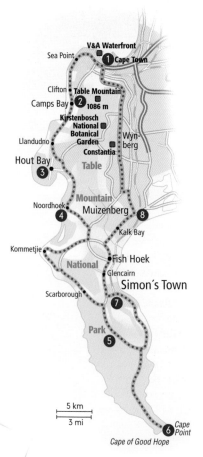

1–2

From Cape Town follow the coast road south through Green Point and Sea Point before it snakes its way through the upmarket residences of Clifton with its famous beaches. Next is Camps Bay, where a stunning swathe of white sand beach is lined by a row of fashionable restaurants and bars, and is backed by the Twelve Apostles. This is one of the most beautiful beaches in the world, although you won't see many people in the ocean – the Atlantic's too cold to swim in.

2–3

After Camps Bay, the mansions stop and the road follows the rocky coast through to Hout Bay, passing the Twelve Apostles Hotel and the upmarket village of Llandudno. Hout Bay is a fishing harbour with another fine beach. You can eat seafood at Mariner's Wharf or visit the fish market. From the harbour, sightseeing boats take passengers to see the Cape fur seal colony on Duiker Island.

3–4

The next section of road is the stunning 15km (9mi) Chapman's Peak Drive, perhaps one of the world's most scenic drives. Now a toll road, it's carved in the rock 600m (1,970ft) above the crashing waves. Giant nets have been constructed above the road to catch falling boulders and it has been fortified, so in places the road cuts into the mountainside and forms an overhang. As you pass Chapman's Peak the view opens up to the vast stretch of beach in Noordhoek.

4–5

The 8km-long (5mi) beach is Noordhoek's greatest attraction. The road then heads inland to Sun Valley where you turn right onto the M65 to Kommetjie, where the beach is always busy with surfers, and Scarborough, a scattering of holiday homes. The road continues on to the entrance to the Table Mountain National Park (Cape of Good Hope Sector) and en route you can stop at an ostrich farm or visit the large souvenir market at the entrance to the park.

The surfers' paradise of Muizenberg on the Cape Peninsula

5–6

Roughly 65km (40mi) from Cape Town, the southern section of the Table Mountain National Park protects the wild flora and fauna of the lower quarter of the Cape Peninsula. You may spot an ostrich, or antelope such as bontebok or giant eland. However, it is not the wildlife, *fynbos* (Afrikaans meaning 'fine bush') vegetation and wonderful isolated beaches that attract hundreds of thousands of visitors to the very southwestern tip of Africa but rather the awe-inspiring landscape and the sense of being in a significant spot. At Cape Point, on the southern tip of the peninsula, there is a parking area, a visitor centre and a restaurant. From here, a steep footpath and a funicular railway ascend to the Cape Point Lighthouse, which offers sweeping ocean views back along False Bay. The 249m-high (817ft) lighthouse dates from 1860, its powerful light has a range 67km (42mi) in clear weather but as it was often shrouded in dense fog, a new lighthouse was built (1919) almost 100m (330ft) lower down. It safeguards the more than 20,000 ships that use the Cape route every year.

6–7

Once back out of the park, the M4 goes back to Cape Town on the eastern coast of the peninsula along False Bay, so named by sailors who confused the bay with Table Bay to the north. Stop at Boulders Beach, a lovely string of sandy beaches surrounded by massive boulders and home to a colony of African penguins. To protect their natural habitat the area has been fenced but there are boardwalks so visitors can get close to the penguins. Next along the M4 is Simon's Town, home to South Africa's naval base, which rather surprisingly was in the hands of the British until as recently as 1957.

7–8

Continue through Fish Hoek with its good beach, and then on to Kalk Bay with its bustling fishing harbour and bohemian atmosphere. The road then winds its way through to Muizenberg, which has a lovely white sand beach and pounding surf. From here it's a short 30-minute drive along the M3 back to Cape Town.

INSIDER TIP In Simon's Town, **Café Pescado** (tel: 021 786 2272; www.pescados.co.za; R–RR) facing Jubilee Square, serves delicious pizzas and Mozambican-style chicken and seafood.

 ✛ 230 B2

Table Mountain National Park (Cape of Good Hope Sector)
☎ 021 780 95 26
🌐 www.sanparks.org
🕐 Oct–Mar daily 6–6; Apr–Sep 7–5 💰 R147

Cape Point Ostrich Farm
✉ M65, 400m from the entrance to the National Park ☎ 021 780 9294
🌐 www.capepoint ostrichfarm.com
🕐 Fri–Wed 9:30–5:30

Boulders Beach
☎ 021 786 2329
🌐 www.sanparks.org
🕐 Dec, Jan 7–7:30; Feb, Mar, Oct, Nov 8–6:30; Apr–Sep 8–5 💰 R76

Route 62

What	Drive
Distance	613km (380mi)
Time	Allow 2 days
Start	Cape Town ⊕ 222 B2
End	Oudtshoorn ⊕ 223 D2

Route 62 is characterised by a semi-desert Karoo landscape and the dramatic mountains that divide the dry interior from the wetter coastal regions.

1–2

From Cape Town drive 50km (30mi) up the N1 to Paarl in the Winelands, where you can visit the KWV House of Fire distillery and try some premium spirits. From here it's a short 9km (6mi) drive along the R303 through more wine estates to the town of Wellington, which is also an important region for the production of dried fruit.

2–3

From Wellington follow the R303 over the switchbacks of the Bain's Kloof Pass. Opened in 1853, this is one of South Africa's greatest engineering feats. Once over the pass, turn left on the R43 and drive 42km (26mi) to Tulbagh via Wolseley.

Lush vineyards in the Cape Winelands region

3–4

Retrace the R43 and after 27km (17mi) turn left on the R303 and continue for 9km (6mi) to Ceres, the capital of South Africa's fruit growing region. Drive south on the R303 for 24km (15mi) and you'll come to a turn-off back to the R43 to Worcester where you could visit the Karoo National Botanical Garden or the open-air museum.

4–5

Head southeast of Worcester on the R60 along many wine cellars in the Breede River Valley. Robertson, 53km (33mi) from

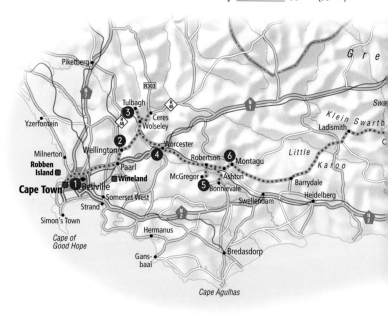

Worcester, has neat streets lined with jacaranda trees with some good restaurants and craft shops, and it is surrounded by wine estates. From Robertson you can choose to go on a short detour to McGregor, home to a number of artists.

5–6

From Robertson, stay on the R60 to go straight to Ashton and Montagu or go on another detour to Bonnievale, 35km (22mi)

along the R317, which is known for its wine and cheese. Loop back round to <u>Montagu</u> and the R62 for about 25km (16mi) via Ashton and the Kogmanskloof Pass. Montagu is famous for its brandy, wine, fruit and natural hot springs; day visitors are welcome in the several pools in the <u>Avalon Springs Resort</u>.

6–7

Follow the R62 to <u>Barrydale</u>, which is dotted with more vineyards and fruit orchards. From Barrydale there's the option of taking a shorter way to the Garden Route via the R324 and Tradouw's Pass, the R322 to Heidelberg and the N2 to Mossel Bay. Alternatively, stay on the R62, for another 77km (48mi) to the <u>Ladismith</u> region, which produces cheese and butter. After another 49km (30mi), you'll reach <u>Calitzdorp</u>, famous for its port, which can be sampled on a couple of estates, and after another 50km (30mi) you'll get to Oudtshoorn, the ostrich capital of the world.

7–8

Get a map from the tourist office in <u>Oudtshoorn</u> and stroll among the lovely old sandstone buildings. There's a string of ostrich farms along the R328 where you can learn all about ostriches and even ride one. 28km (17mi) north from Oudtshoorn are the <u>Cango Caves</u> with fascinating limestone formations.

INSIDER TIP ▶ Perhaps the oddest place to stop is the **Ronnie's Sex Shop** (tel: 028 572 1153; www.ronniessexshop. co.za; R), a roadside pub between Ladismith and Barrydale.

⊕ www.route62.co.za

KWV House of Fire
♁ 230 C4 ✉ Kohler St, Paarl ☎ 021 807 3007 ⊕ www.kwvhouseoffice. co.za ① Tours: Mon–Fri 11:30 and 2:30 ✦ R120

Avalon Springs Resort
♁ 222 C2 ✉ Uitvlucht Street, Montagu
☎ 023 614 1150
⊕ www.avalonsprings. co.za ① Daily 8–8
✦ R60–R130 depending on the day

Cango Caves
♁ 223 D2 (Oudtshoorn)
✉ R328 ☎ 044 272 7410
⊕ www.cango-caves. co.za ① Daily tours every hour 9–4
✦ R110–R165 depending on tour

Panorama Route

What	Drive
Distance	127km (80mi)
Time	1 day
Start	Sabie ✚ 229 E3
End	Blyde River Canyon ✚ 229 E4

The Panorama Route winds through the scenic mountainous highlands that overlook the lowveld region and the southern Kruger National Park.

1–2

Drive along the R532 from <u>Sabie</u> for 29km (18mi) to Graskop where there are a series of waterfalls to visit. The Sabie Falls plunge 73m (240ft) down Sabie Gorge and the 65m (213ft) <u>Mac Mac Falls</u> drop into a series of refreshing pools that you can splash around in. Once in <u>Graskop</u>, a 1.5km (1mi) detour on the R533 toward Hazyview takes you to the Panorama Gorge and Falls, the location of the Big Swing, a cable gorge swing with a 68m (223ft) drop.

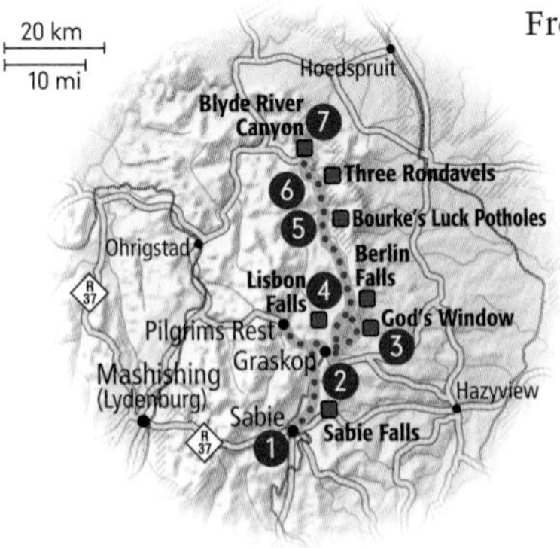

2–3

From Graskop follow the R533, 15km (9mi) to <u>Pilgrim's Rest</u>. The village is a living museum dedicated to the gold mining era. Park in the top parking area (you'll see the tour buses) and explore the single street of restored miners' cottages, duck into the museums, have a go at gold panning or visit the shops and restaurants.

3–4

Retrace your steps back through <u>Graskop</u> and follow the R532 again, north toward the <u>Blyde River Canyon</u>. <u>Pinnacle Rock</u>, a 30m (98ft) free-standing quartzite buttress, and God's Window, the first of several viewpoints, are 6km (4mi) and 9km (6mi) respectively north of Graskop on the R534, a scenic loop off the R532. God's Window offers unparalleled views from the edge of the escarpment over the lowveld and Kruger 900m (2,950ft) below, and a little further on, Wonder View has another sweeping view.

4–5

Where the R534 rejoins the R532, turn left back toward Graskop for 800m (872 yards) and then right on to a gravel road for 2.2km (1.4mi to the 92m (302ft) Lisbon Falls. Head north again on the R532 and 2km (1mi) after the R534 turn-off turn left to reach the car park for the 45m (148ft) Berlin Falls.

Lisbon Falls, the highest waterfall in the region

5–6

Next is Bourke's Luck Potholes, 35km (22mi) north of Graskop at the confluence of the Blyde and Treur rivers, where waterborne sand and rock have scoured out huge cylindrical potholes into the river bed.

6–7

Another 20km (12mi) brings you to the Three Rondavels viewpoint with spectacular views of the Blyde River Canyon. The Blyde River snakes its way down to sparkling Blydespoort Dam at the bottom with the shimmering lowveld plains beyond. The 26km-long (16mi) Blyde River Canyon is the largest canyon in southern Africa, and the highlight of this tour. From here you can retrace your steps back to Graskop, Sabie or to the canyon's southern exit.

INSIDER TIP ▶ Stop off at **Harrie's Pankcakes** (p. 158) on Graskop's main road for a pancake or a slice of home-made cake.

Swaziland

What	Drive
Distance	200km (124mi)
Time	2 days
Start	Ngwenya/Oshoek Border Post on the N17, Mpumalanga ✛ 229 E2
End	Lavumisa Border Post 11km (7mi) from the N2, KwaZulu-Natal ✛ 229 E2

A panoramic view of the landscape near Mbabane

The smallest country in the southern hemisphere and one still ruled by a royal family, the tiny autonomous kingdom of Swaziland lies almost entirely within South Africa, the landscape is dominated by bush and mountains. If you drive to Swaziland from South Africa you will need a letter of authorization from your car rental company (cross border fee) as proof of insurance. You can use South African Rand in Swaziland, and you will be required to produce a passport when you enter and exit the kingdom.

1–2

At the border crossing at <u>Ngwenya/Oshoek</u>, formalities should take no longer than 30 minutes. Stop at Ngwenya

Glass (daily 9–4; www.ngwenyaglass.co.sz) in Motjane, 5km (3mi) from the border, where you can buy hand-blown items such as glasses, vases and statues of African animals and watch glass blowers. A number of other crafts are for sale too. From here it's a short 18km (11mi) drive to the country's sleepy capital, Mbabane.

2–3

There's not much to see in Mbabane's busy grid of bland, functional buildings but do stop at the Swazi Market at the end of Allister Miller Street for its colourful display of fresh produce and curios. The main road leaves town on a dramatic and giddy descent down into the Ezulwini Valley where the road winds in a series of sweeping curves for approximately 10km (6mi).

3–4

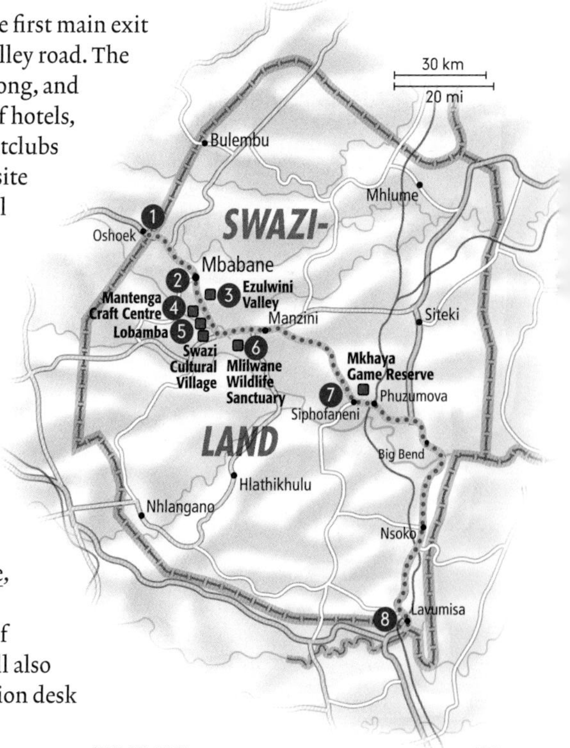

At the bottom, take the first main exit to the old Ezulwini Valley road. The valley is 28km (17mi) long, and is home to a number of hotels, restaurants, bars, nightclubs and attractions. Opposite the Ezulwini Sun hotel is the Swazi Health and Beauty Studio (tel: 268 416 1164; daily 6–6), best known for its large outdoor pool fed by a warm spring known as the Cuddle Puddle. About 4km (3mi) further on is the Mantenga Craft Centre, which is an attractive purpose-built village of craft shops where you'll also find a tourist information desk and a desk for Swazi Trails, which can arrange white-water rafting, caving, hiking and safaris into the parks.

4–5

Just past the craft centre is the entrance to the small Mantenga Nature Reserve with picnic spots and walking paths to the 95m (312ft) Mantenga Falls. Also within the reserve is the Swazi Cultural Village, which is a living, working reconstruction of a 19th-century Swazi village with traditional grass beehive huts, where you may see food being prepared, crafts being made, and livestock

A traditional beehive hut at the Swazi Cultural Village

wandering around. The entrance fee to the village includes local guides to show you around.

5–6

In the heart of the valley at Lobamba and 20km (12mi) from Mbabane, are Swaziland's Houses of Parliament and the royal residence of Ludzidzini, home to King Mswati III and his Queen Mother, or *Ndlovukazi*, meaning "she-elephant". These can't be visited but next door is the National Museum, which covers the history of Swaziland and the royal family and there are some wonderful old photographs.

6–7

Take the right turning from the Ezulwini Valley road just after Ludzidzini and after 3.5km (2mi) on a dirt road is the entrance gate to Mlilwane Wildlife Sanctuary. You can go on guided game drives, mountain-bike trails, horseback rides or simply walk through the grasslands that are home to white rhino, antelope, buffalo, hippo, crocodile and many species of birds. Stay overnight here, as there's a variety of accommodation to choose from and a delightful restaurant overlooking a hippo pool where the staff entertains with singing and dancing each evening.

7–8

From Mlilwane, drive on the new highway 19km (12mi) to Manzini, but don't linger in the dull and scruffy town, just continue straight through. After 8km (5mi) the road splits, take the right-hand turn and continue for 44km (27mi) to the gate of the Mkhaya Game Reserve, home to rhino, elephant and numerous antelope. Private cars are not allowed into the reserve, so aim to get to the gate by 10am to park and meet your guide for the 6-hour excursion into the reserve. Game drives and a generous lunch are included and it's essential to pre-arrange this tour. From Mkhaya it's 91km (56mi) to the border post at Lavumisa and Maputaland (p. 98) in KwaZulu-Natal.

INSIDER TIP The **Maguga Viewpoint Restaurant** (near Piggs Peak at the Maguga Dam, 40km (25mi) north of Mbabane; tel: 268 668 6637; R) is a good place to stop on the scenic loop road. The terrace has lovely views over the water and the food is freshly prepared.

Mantenga Nature Reserve
✉ Mantenga Craft Centre
☎ 268 416 1151 🔖 R120

National Museum
✉ Lobamba
☎ 263 416 1516
🌐 www.sntc.org.sz
🕐 Mon–Fri 8–4:30, Sat, Sun 10–4
🔖 R100

Mlilwane Wildlife Sanctuary
☎ 268 528 3943
🌐 www.biggameparks.org
🔖 R50

Mkhaya Game Reserve
☎ 268 528 3943
🌐 www.biggameparks.org
🕐 Daily 10–4
🔖 R735 day safari

On an informative guided walk with armed park guides near
the camp Berg-En-Dal in the southern Kruger National Park

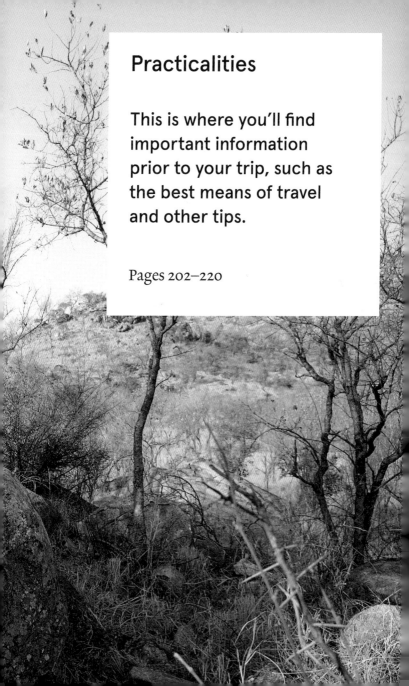

Practicalities

This is where you'll find important information prior to your trip, such as the best means of travel and other tips.

BEFORE YOU GO

Advance Information
South African Tourism: www.southafrica.net

UK & Ireland
Second Floor, 1-2 Castle Lane,
London, SW1E6DR
Tel: 208 971 9350

In the US
500 Fifth Avenue, Suite 2200,
New York, NY10110
Tel: 212 730 2929

In Australia
Level 1, 117 York Street, Sydney, NSW 2000
Tel: 029 261 5000

Websites
www.portfoliocollection.com
Carefully selected accommodation in all
price categories – a leader in South African
booking portals

www.weathersa.co.za
Weather forecasts from the national
meteorological service

www.sanparks.org
Official website of South African Nation
Parks with detailed descriptions of the
protected conservation areas, as well as
online booking options

Provincial Websites
http://goto.capetown
www.zulu.org.za
www.mpumalanga.com
www.golimpopo.com
http://freestatetourism.org
www.tourismnorthwest.co.za
http://experiencenortherncape.com
www.gauteng.net
www.visiteasterncape.co.za

Concessions
Discounts for certain tickets (museums,
exhibitions and nature reserves) are only
valid for South African residents. Other
concessions apply to:
Children Most hotels offer adjoining rooms
or discounts for children sharing their
parents' room and there is plenty of family
self-catering accommodation, especially in
the parks. There are discounts to museums
and attractions though age ranges vary.
Students Holders of an International
Student Identity Card (ISIC) or a Youth
Hostel Association (YHA) card can get
reductions on long-distance buses, the
Baz Bus (hop-on-hop-off backpackers'
bus) and some backpackers' hostels. Cards
are not broadly recognised elsewhere but
it's always worth asking.
Senior Citizens Discounts on entry fees
and transport are offered to the over-60s.
Proof of age required.

Customs
Duty-free allowances are up to R3,000
worth of gifts, 50ml of perfume, 250ml eau
de toilette, 2 litres of wine or 1 litre spirits,
and 200 cigarettes, 50 cigars or 250g of
tobacco.
When returning to home, make sure that
you are aware of the regulations of your
customs authority.

Currency & Foreign Exchange
South Africa's **currency** is the Rand, denoted
with an R on banknotes and price tags. Coins
are issued in denominations of 5, 10, 20 and
50 cents, R1, R2 and R5. Notes (bills) are
R10, R20, R50, R100 and R200. Try to avoid
accumulating R200 notes as many forgeries
are in circulation and an increasing number
of retailers refuse to take them. A maximum
of R5,000 in South African notes can be
imported or exported.
Traveller's cheques and cash can be **ex-
changed** in any bank where you can also
withdraw cash from a credit card.
Transactions are subject to a commission
charge. Branches of American Express and
Rennies (local agent for Thomas Cook)
can be found in the large shopping malls
and airports.

Exchange rates:
R100 ≈ £5.3   £1 ≈ 18.7 R
R100 ≈ €7   €1 ≈ R14.5

ATMs are prolific in banks, petrol stations and shopping malls in the urban areas, but less so in remote areas.

Credit and debit cards are widely acceptable in shops, restaurants and hotels, and a credit (not debit) card is essential if you are renting a car. The exception is petrol (gas), which can often only be paid fo in cash. Many petrol (gas) stations have ATMs but this cannot always be relied upon. Increasingly the chip-and-pin system is being used for foreign credit cards.

Electricity
The power supply in South Africa is 220/230 volts. Sockets accept three-prong round-pin plugs. An international adaptor is needed for two-prong or three-prong flat-pin plugs, you can either buy one locally or ask at the hotel front desk.

Embassies & High Commissions
Australian High Commission, Pretoria
292 Orient St, Arcadia, Pretoria
Tel: +27 (012) 423 6000
https://southafrica.embassy.gov.au

British High Commission, Pretoria
255 Hill St, Arcadia, Pretoria
Tel: +27 (012) 421 7500
www.gov.uk/world/south-africa

British Consulate General, Cape Town
15th Floor, Norton Rose House,
8 Riebeek Street, Foreshore, Cape Town
Tel: +27 (021) 405 2400

Canadian High Commission, Pretoria
1103 Arcadia Street, Hatflield, Pretoria
Tel: +27 (012) 422 3000
www.canadainternational.gc.ca

Embassy of Ireland, Pretoria
570 Fehrsen St, Brooklyn, Pretoria
Tel: +27 (012) 452 1000
www.dfa.ie/irish-embassy/south-africa

U.S. Embassy, Pretoria
877 Pretorius St, Arcadia, Pretoria
Tel: +27 (012) 431 4000
https://za.usembassy.gov

U.S. Consulate General, Cape Town
2 Reddam Ave, Steenberg Estate,
Cape Town
Tel: +27 (021) 702 7300

U.S. Consulate General, Durban
303 Dr Pixley Kaseme St,
Durban Central, Durban
Tel: +27 (031) 305 7600

U.S. Consulate General, Johannesburg
1 Sandton Dr, Sandhurst, Johannesburg
Tel: +27 (011) 290 3000

Health
Insurance
Medical treatment in South Africa must be paid for and you will be asked to show proof of payment before treatment. Travel insurance is essential and should include repatriation to your home country.

Medical Care
The standard of health care provided by private doctors and clinics in the urban areas is excellent. In an emergency, even the underfunded and busy government clinics will offer good medical care. However, doctors and medical facilities in rural areas are scarce.

Malaria
Most of South Africa is malaria-free. Before you travel, research the malaria risk areas (such as the Kruger National Park) and consult your doctor or a travel clinic for up-to-date advice.
If you plan to visit a malaria area during a high-risk season, you will be prescribed anti-malaria tablets or a standby oral prophylaxis. Once in the malaria area, be sure to use mosquito repellents, wear long pants and long-sleeved shirts or blouses, and sleep under a mosquito net.

Weather

Even in winter the sun can be very intense, so bring sunglasses, hat and high-factor sunscreen.

Medication:

Staff in pharmacies can offer medical advice, though for prescriptions you will need to visit a doctor. Bring sufficient supplies of regular medication or note down the generic name as it may be sold under another brand in South Africa.

Safe Water

Tap water is safe to drink and bottled water is widely available and reasonably priced.

National Holidays

1 January	New Year's Day
21 March	Human Rights Day
March/April	Good Friday
March/April	Family Day (Easter Mon)
27 April	Freedom Day
1 May	Workers' Day
16 June	Youth Day
9 August	Women's Day
24 September	Heritage Day
16 December	Day of Reconciliation
25 December	Christmas Day
26 December	Day of Goodwill

Whenever any public holiday falls on a Sunday, the Monday following on it is a public holiday.

Personal Safety

South Africa's cities in particular have a problem with theft and isolated incidents of car-jacking. Tourists may be specifically targeted so keep an eye on who's around you, avoid isolated places and dangerous hotspots, and try not to leave your vehicle unattended.

Carry money in a slim belt under your clothes.

Make use of hotel safes for valuables.

Don't flash your wealth and leave expensive jewellery at home.

Avoid walking at night.

Don't leave bags or other items visible in your car.

Drive with windows closed and doors locked.

Be careful when drawing money at ATMs. Assume that anybody who comes too close or offers to help you has sinister motives. On shopping or other excursions, carry only as much cash as you are likely to need for the day.

Make a note of your credit and debit card details and any emergency numbers and keep this separate from the actual cards, if your card does go missing then have it cancelled immediately!

Staying In Touch
Post

Post offices are identified by a red, white and blue envelope sign and post boxes are usually red pillar boxes. Opening hours are Mon–Fri 9–3:30 and Sat 9–11 (longer in the shopping malls and airports).

Postage rates can be found at www.post office.co.za (international post cards: R7.90, international letters: R9.15).

Public Telephones

Card and coin phones are widely available, and you can dial direct internationally from them. Phone cards are available from supermarkets and small shops. All telephone numbers in South Africa are composed of a three digit area code and a seven digit number. You must always use the area code, even if phoning from within the area.

International Dialling Codes

South Africa	0027
UK:	0044
USA/Canada:	001
Irish Republic:	00353
Australia:	0061
New Zealand:	0064

Mobile phone providers and services

MTN, Vodacom and Cell C provide network coverage in urban areas and along most trunk routes, but not in the more remote game reserves. If you expect to phone or text home regularly, consider buying a local SIM card, as call rates are much cheaper than for international roaming.

WiFi and internet
Inexpensive internet cafés can be found in all towns, although they may close over weekends, and most hotels and lodges catering to international visitors have ADSL and/or WiFi access.

Emergency Numbers

Police (landline/mobile)	☎ 10111
Emergency Call Centre (mobile)	☎ 112
Ambulance (landline/mobile)	☎ 10177

Time
South Africa Standard Time (SAST) is two hours ahead of Greenwich Mean Time (GMT+2). Between March to October, when **daylight saving** is observed in the UK, South Africa is only one hour ahead of the UK.

Travel Documents
For entry into South Africa you will need a passport that is valid for at least 30 days beyond your date of entry (90 days for Lesotho and six months for Swaziland). In most instances, you will also need a return or onward ticket at the time of entry. Most foreign nationals are allowed 90 days visa-free entry but you should confirm your visa requirements with your travel agency prior to departure.To rent a vehicle, you will need a credit card and a valid the national driver's license; some car rental companies also require an International License.

When to Go
The **Western** and **Eastern Capes** generally have dry, warm summers and cool, wet winters. The Indian Ocean coast along **KwaZulu-Natal** is tropical with relatively warm temperatures all year, while inland **Johannesburg and the north** have mild dry winters and wet summers. Do note, how-

ever, that while temperatures follow a similar pattern around the country, with November to February being the warmest months and June, July and August the coolest. The dry winter months (May-October) are best for **game viewing**, during this time the animals are easier to spot in the sparse bush and they also congregate at waterholes. Book well in advance for the long summer **school holidays** over December as this is the most popular month for local tourism.

GETTING THERE

South Africa has international airports in **Johannesburg, Cape Town and Durban, which are served by numerous airlines. Most of the other larger cities are connected by domestic flights with airlines such as South African Airways (www.flysaa.com).**

From the UK
Carriers include British Airways (www.britishairways.com), Virgin (www.virgin-atlantic.com), and South African Airways (www.flysaa.com).

From the Rest of Europe
Carriers include Air France, TAP Portugal, Alitalia, Austrian Airlines, Iberia, Lufthansa, KLM, and Swiss International. There are also indirect flights from other airlines such as Kenya Airways, Ethiopian Airlines, Air Namibia and Emirates.

From the US and Canada
Delta and South African Airways both fly directly between the USA and South Africa. American Airlines code shares with British Airways on flights to South Africa via London.

From Australia and New Zealand
Qantas code shares with South African Airways from Sydney and Perth, Singapore Airlines flies from Sydney and Wellington via Singapore, and Malaysia Airlines flies from several Australian cities and Auckland in New Zealand via Kuala Lumpur.

FIRST TWO HOURS

Scheduled international flights arrive at the three gateway airports listed below, from where there are onward domestic and regional flights. They offer food courts, banks and exchange bureaux, mobile phone, wireless and SIM card rental desks and postal services.

Ground Transport Fees:

R	under R100
RR	R100–R300
RRR	over R300

Arriving in Johannesburg
OR Tambo International Airport (JNB) (formerly Johannesburg International) is the main point of entry into South Africa. It lies 24km (15mi) from the city centre and 35km (22mi) from the northern suburbs (tel: 086 727 7888; www.airports.co.za). Metered **taxis** (RRR) are found outside the arrivals hall and take 45 minutes to 1 hour to hotels in the northern suburbs.

To book one of the cheaper **shuttle buses** (RRR) to the northern suburbs go to the desks in the arrivals hall.

The most convenient way to get to Johannesburg and Pretoria is with the safe and modern **Gautrain** (RR; www.gautrain.co.za).

Many of the large hotels offer their own **pick-up service**.

Car rental desks in the Parkade Centre include Avis, Budget, Europcar, Hertz, Imperial and Tempest/Sixt.

Gauteng Tourism Authority has a desk in the international terminal (tel: 011 390 3602/14; www.gauteng.net; daily 8–10).

Arriving in Cape Town
Cape Town International Airport (CPT) is the second major point of entry to South Africa for international visitors. It lies 22km (14mi) east of the city centre along the N2 highway (tel: 082 727 7888; www.airports.co.za).

Metered **taxis** (RRR) can be found outside and take 30–45 minutes into the city centre (Touch Down Taxis are officially authorised; tel: 083 652 0786).

Shuttle buses (RR) can be arranged in international arrivals from Citi Hopper (tel: 082 773 7678; www.citihopper.co.za) or pre-arranged through Centurion Tours (tel: 082 472 6216; www.centurion tours.co.za).

Car rental desks in the international and domestic arrivals terminals include Avis, Budget, Europcar, Hertz, Imperial and Tempest/Sixt.

Cape Town Tourism has a desk in international arrivals (tel: 021 934 1949) and at The Pinnacle, corner of Berg and Castle streets (tel: 021 487 6800; www.capetown.travel; Mon–Fri 8–6, Sat, Sun 9–1).

Arriving in Durban (DUR)
King Shaka International Airport is about 35km (20mi) north of the city centre (tel: 086 727 7888; www.airports.co.za). **Taxis** (RR) wait outside the terminal for transfers to the city centre.

Shuttle buses (RRR) can be called from Airport Bus Shuttle Service (tel: 031 465 5573; https://shuttle.airportbustransport.co.za).

Car rental desks in the international and domestic arrivals terminals include Avis, Budget, Europcar, Hertz, Imperial and Tempest/Sixt.

Durban Tourism has a small desk in domestic arrivals (tel: 031 304 7500; 7am–9pm) and downtown (90 Florida Road; tel: 031 322 4146; www.durban experience.co.za; Mon–Fri 8–5, Sat, Sun 9–1).

GETTING AROUND

South Africa has an excellent network of transport and highways, and you can travel between regions quickly and easily – be it by car, bus, train or plane.

Domestic Air Travel

There is an efficient network of domestic flights linking the main cities, none of which are more than two hours' flying time apart. Good deals can be had if you book early through the websites. Some of the private game reserves and lodges can arrange flights to their own airstrips.

British Airways' (BA) South African operator, **Comair** (www.comair.co.za), links the larger domestic cities as well as destinations in other southern African countries.

Also owned by Comair is **Kulula** (www.kulula.com), a no-frills airline linking major domestic cities and other African cities on a code share agreement with BA.

Budget airlines **Mango** (www.flymango.com) and **FlySafair** (www.flysafair.co.za) have competitive fares.

Federal Air (tel: 011 395 9000; www.fedair.com) operates daily flights between Johannesburg and all the top game lodges in and around Kruger National Park.

South African Airways covers the whole country and other southern African cities in conjunction with their subsidiaries SA Airlink and SA Express (www.flysaa.com).

Trains

Regional

Passenger services connecting Johannesburg to Cape Town, Durban, Port Elisabeth and East London as well as Cape Town to Queenstown are operated by the **Passenger**

Insider Info
Journey on the Blue Train

The legendary Blue Train has tinted pan-oramic windows that showcase South Africa's magnificent scenery and land-scapes. It is a 5-star hotel on rails and the spacious and luxurious compartments have private bathrooms and digital enter-tainment systems. In the evening, dinner is served in the opulent dining car where guests enjoy exquisite food and fine drinks. In the afternoon, high tea (or ice-cold champagne) is served in style in the lounge saloon car. A Blue Train journey is the real highlight of an eventful stay in South Africa.

Rail Agency of South Africa under the name of **Shosholoza Meyl**. Services are reasonably comfortable and affordable but slow.

There are sitting and sleeper compartments, and on the Johannesburg–Cape Town and Johannesburg–Durban route there is also the option to transport private motor vehicles. Fast food can be bought in the dining car.

Booking, enquiries and reservations are best directed to tel: 011 773 6566 (Gauteng), tel: 021 449 2124 (Western Cape), tel: 031 361 8227 (Durban), tel: 041 994 2002 (Eastern Cape), and tel: 051 408 2262 (Free State) or online www.shosholozameyl.co.za.

Local

Spoornet operates **Metrorail** (www.metro rail.co.za) in the bigger cities of Gauteng, KwaZulu-Natal, Eastern and Western Cape, linking the city centres with the suburbs used by commuters. It's not advised for visitors to use these because of the high risk of crime.

A safer option is Gauteng's **Gautrain** (www.gautrain.co.za), a high-speed rail link connecting OR Tambo International Airport to the upmarket suburb of Sandton and links to central Pretoria and Johannesburg.

Luxury trains

PRASA operates weekly **Premier Classe** from Jo'Burg to Cape Town and Durban (www.southafricanrailways.co.za). Considerably more upmarket than the regular train, it has good food and service. Compartments sleep 2–4 (tourist class) and 1–2 (premier class) and quality meals are served in the dining car.

South Africa's famous **Blue Train** (www. bluetrain.co.za) has scheduled departures between Pretoria and Cape Town via Johannesburg and between Pretoria and Hoedspruit/Kruger National Park, and there are other special excursions throughout the year (p. 209). Spacious suites with baths and digital entertain-ment help it live up to its reputation as a 5-star hotel on wheels.

A similar luxury train, **The Pride of Africa**, operated by Rovos Rail (www.rovos.com), also runs luxury trips to Mpumalanga and to several countries to the north of South Africa.

Buses

A number of companies run **long-distance bus** services with air-conditioning, toilets, and on-board refreshments. Three main operators cover dozens of daily routes. Among them are **Greyhound** (tel: 011 611 8000; www.greyhound.co.za); **Intercape** (tel: 021 380 4400; www.intercape.co.za); and **Intercity Express** (tel: 087 150 1895; www.intercityexpress.co.za).

Some distances are long, however, and many buses travel overnight and could deposit you at your destination at an inconvenient hour. Consider too, that if you book early enough online, airfares with the no-frills airlines are comparable to bus tickets. Bus tickets can be booked online through South Africa's nationwide reservations service **Computicket** (www.computicket.co.za).

The jump-on-jump-off **Baz Bus** (tel: 021 422 52 02; www.bazbus.com) picks up and drops off at backpackers' hostels. It's cheaper over short distances than regular bus companies and doesn't arrive in the middle of the night. It runs along the coast between Cape Town and Durban and between Durban and Johannesburg – with short detours to visit tourist attractions.

The cities operate **local buses** along major roads with clearly signposted stops. In Johannesburg these are run by **Metrobus** (www.mbus.co.za); in Cape Town **Golden Arrow** (www.gabs.co.za) and in Durban **Muvo** (www.muvo.co.za). A short journey will cost less than R10.

Taxis

Taxis cannot be hailed on the street and must be ordered by phone; any hotel or restaurant can do this and they turn up quickly. They are metered but not cheap; expect to pay around R75 for 3–4km (2–3mi). Larger groups and wheelchair users should ask for a Toyota Venture, which has extra seats. It is usual to tip taxi drivers 10 per cent.

Minibus taxis are a popular form of local transport and are hailed down at the side of the street. Like the Metrorail, however, they are not advised for tourists as there is the danger of theft and they are often driven recklessly.

Driving

Driving is the easiest and most flexible way of getting around South Africa. A network of excellent highways links the major cities.

National highways

The N1 runs from the Zimbabwe border in the north to Cape Town via Johannesburg, Pretoria and Bloemfontein. Durban is linked to Johannesburg by the N3 and to Cape Town by the coastal N2 via East London, Port Elizabeth and the Garden Route. Maputo in Mozambique is linked to Gaborone in Botswana via Johannesburg by the N4, while the N7 runs up the western coast and links Cape Town with Windhoek in Namibia. Tolls are charged so keep some cash handy.

Secondary roads

There's a comprehensive network of other roads across the country. Almost all are tarred but in some rural areas they are unsealed, though usually in good condition. Roads in **Kruger National Park** are mostly tarred and suitable for a normal car.

Safety

When **driving in cities**, be aware of where the trouble spots are – inner city areas, townships, neglected neighbourhoods – where it's not advised to drive. Carry a good map and mobile phone, and if driving at night keep doors locked and windows up.

Almost all hotels, tourist attractions and shopping malls have adequate **parking**. If parking on the street, make use of **car guards** who are usually identified by a badge or work vest and pay them R2–R5 on your return for watching your vehicle. Always lock your vehicle and never leave anything on display. In the event of a roadside **break-down** contact your car hire company.

Driving Essentials

Drive on the **left-hand side** of the road. Overtaking is on the right but on the highways be careful of other cars overtaking on the right. **Road signs** are in English and Afrikaans. **Four-way stops** are common and are indicated by red stop signs. Whoever gets to the junction first (including pedestrians) has right of way, then the others get their respective turns.

At traffic lights, a **flashing green** arrow lets you turn across or off a highway while straight over is still on red. Traffic lights in South Africa are known as **robots** and roundabouts as **traffic circles**.

Speed limits are 60kph (37mph) on urban roads, 80–100kph (50–62mph) outside built up areas, and 120kph (74mph) on highways. Speed traps and cameras are common. Drivers are required by law to wear **seatbelts** and to make use of **hands-free kits**. Driving under the influence is a serious offence, and the **blood alcohol limit** is less than 0.05g per 100ml of blood.

In urban areas **petrol stations** (gas stations) are plentiful and are open long hours but in remote parts remember to fill up when you can. Some **petrol stations** only accept cash **and not credit cards**, although most have ATMs.

All roads are numbered. **National highways** are denoted with an N, **municipal highways** with an M, other **major roads** with an R, and **minor dirt roads** with a D.

Car Rental

Anyone over 21 (25 with some companies) can hire a car with their licence from their home country as long as it's in English. Holders of licences in other languages will need an International Driving Licence. Additionally you'll need your passport and a credit card.

All the international car hire companies have offices at the airports and in the cities where you can hire a car immediately. Most will let you return the car to other cities but this must be agreed in advance and will attract a surcharge.

ACCOMMODATION

Expect to pay in high season per double room per night

R	under R1,500
RR	R1,500–R3,000
RRR	over R3,000

Backpacker Hostels

Hostels are found in the popular destinations, especially along the coast. They offer dormitory-style accommodation and double rooms. Facilities are likely to include a kitchen, pool or garden, and the management can usually arrange activities and transport within the local area. Some rent out surfboards or mountain bikes and arrange their own excursions. *Coast to Coast* (www.coastingafrica.com) is an annual guidebook to South Africa's hostels available free from the hostels.

Bed-and-Breakfasts

Even the smallest town has a private home with rooms available. A home-away-from-home atmosphere is usually the norm and most are owner-operated. If you prefer more anonymity, some have separate entrances or rooms in garden cottages. A Continental or full English breakfast is included. Visit www.bnbfinder.co.za.

Guest Houses

Some guest houses are in period homes or historic buildings, and in most a great deal of thought has gone into the furnishings; extras can include swimming pools or air-conditioning. Breakfast is included in the rates, and in some, evening meals are available on request. Contact the **Guest House Association of South Africa** (www.ghasa.co.za).

Hotels

Large **international chains** such as Holiday Inn, Hilton and Intercontinental are well represented and there's a growing crop of luxury and boutique hotels set in stunning locations. **Protea Hotels** (http://protea.marriott.com) manage a range of 3- to 4-star individually designed hotels, while the modern **City Lodge** chain (www.citylodge.co.za) is popular with business travellers. Smaller towns usually feature at least one 2- to 3-star hotel.

Luxury Game Lodges

These are usually located in **private game reserves** and are all-inclusive of meals and game drives and some have extras such as a spa. The highlight is to sleep in close proximity to the wildlife in luxurious surroundings. Some are isolated and accessed by light aircraft.

National Parks Accommodation

Self-catering cottages, chalets and campsites can be found in the **restcamps** of the larger national parks and reserves such as Kruger or the uKhahlamba-Drakensberg. There's usually a central block where reception, a shop, and perhaps a swimming pool or restaurant are located. At some, additional game drives and walks are on offer. In the smaller game reserves a couple of cottages may be available but with few facilities and you'll have to take everything such as linen with you.

Self-catering

Self-contained flats, cottages or chalets are widely available and for groups or families, rates are economical. Some are individually located, or are in blocks of flats; others are in large resorts with campsites and recreational facilities. Most towns have municipal campsites which usually also have a few chalets.

Right: There are numerous beautifully appointed lodges in and around the national parks, including this Zulu-inspired hut

Around the campfire at Punda Maria Rest Camp, in the northern Kruger National Park

Parks accommodation is managed by **South African National Parks** (www.sanparks.org), **Cape Nature** (www.capenature.co.za), or **KZN Wildlife** (www.kznwildlife.com), and should be booked well in advance especially during local school holidays.

Finding a Room

It's advisable to **reserve your room in advance**, particularly in the parks, and on the coast during the long South African school holidays in December.

In the parks always enquire about room availability at the gate first to avoid travelling long distances before finding out that there's no room to stay at a restcamp. **The Portfolio Collection** offers a wide range of accommodation in all price categories (www.portfoliocollection.com).

Room Rates

Rates vary tremendously from around R100 for a dorm bed in a backpacker's

hostel to over R10,000 in a super-luxurious game lodge. In most places rates stay the same throughout the year. The exception to this is on the coast where prices increase dramatically during summer. Some establishments offer a discount for booking online. Selected accommodation is listed in the Where to... section of individual chapters.

FOOD AND DRINK

Expect to pay for a two-course meal per person excluding drinks:

R	under R200
RR	R200–R350
RRR	over R350

Cafés

Cafés are **open throughout the day** and focus on breakfasts, coffees and light meals, although they still offer a full range of alcoholic drinks. Some close earlier in the evening than the restaurants while others pump up their menus and become full-on bars as the day wears on. In a potentially confusing quirk of South African English the term café is more often used to describe a small convenience store than a place to eat.

Ethnic Cuisine

In Cape Town you will find restaurants serving Cape Malay cuisine (cooked in spices and dried fruit); while Durban is famous for its Indian food, especially bunny chow – half a loaf of bread with the middle scooped out and filled with curry. One of the most popular and social ways to eat in South Africa is the *braai*; most households have one, and every weekend friends meet to cook over the coals.

Local Produce

The South African climate is ideal for agriculture and just about every imaginable fruit and vegetable is grown. The variety of meat on offer is just as extensive and includes prime steak, Karoo lamb and game meat such as ostrich and kudu. Specialities include *biltong* (dried salted meat) and *boerewors* (a coarse, fat sausage). *Pap* is a stiff maize porridge, while *bobotie* is a spicy local version of shepherd's pie with a savoury custard topping. Seafood is plentiful along the coast, and most menus feature "linefish" (catch of the day).

Restaurants

Many restaurants enjoy lovely settings or fine views. South Africa doesn't have pubs as such; so most restaurants double up as bars, too. There are a number of chain establishments that lack individuality but are good value. South Africans are fairly casual when dining out and generally nowhere requires a jacket and tie.

Practicalities

Chain restaurants and cafés are open for breakfast until 10pm, while most res-

Delicious seafood meal

taurants open from noon until midnight, though some close for a couple of hours between lunch and dinner. Some close one day a week, usually Sunday or Monday. In the smaller towns, hours are shorter and kitchens usually close by 9pm.

It's always a good idea to **make a reservation** at the popular places but apart from weekends you shouldn't have to wait too long for a table.

Almost all establishments accept **credit cards**.

Service is generally of a high calibre. Tables usually have a dedicated waiter and, as **tip money** makes up a substantial

Jazz session in Johannesburg's Newtown district

part of their income, a voluntary tip of 10 to 15 per cent of the bill is the norm.

Where to Eat
There's a thriving restaurant scene and there are several sources of information. Once in South Africa look out for the annual *Eat Out* magazine (www.eatout.co.za), or visit www.dining-out.co.za or www.restaurants.co.za.

What to Drink
Wine is available and, as it's produced in the Cape Winelands, there's a wide choice of affordable labels. The most widely available white wines are Chardonnay, great with fish and seafood, and the crisper, fruitier Sauvignon Blanc, which perfectly complements spicy Cape Malay dishes and curries. Of the reds, the full-bodied Cabernet Sauvignon and the more keenly priced Pinotage are the most popular. South African Breweries produce a range o good bottled lagers, and look out for Windhoek Lager from Namibia. Few places have **beer** on tap and British-style ales are not available.

There's a full range of **spirits**, including several home-grown brandies and South African Amarula, a cream-based liqueur made from the fruit of the Marula tree. Supermarkets are legally only allowed to sell wine. Other alcohol is sold in bottle stores, usually next to the supermarkets. No alcohol is sold from shops on Sundays.

ENTERTAINMENT

The arts and nightlife in the cities cover a broad range of genres, from theatres and casinos to traditional dancing and township jazz. In the rural areas, however, entertainment is limited to drinking in a local bar. For listings and online booking, visit Computicket (www.com puticket.com).

Nightlife
The cities have numerous late-night bars and **nightclubs** varying from fashionably smart to student grunge. Most attract an entry charge of around R50 and open until at least 2–3 in the morning. As well as mainstream dance music, jazz and Kwaito (South African hip-hop) are popular too. Check national and local newspapers for listings.

The many large **casino** resorts also have cinemas, show bars and a selection of nightclubs.

While rural South Africa is fairly conservative in its attitude, there are many **gay and lesbian venues** in the three liberal big cities.

SHOPPING

Opening Hours
Shops in **malls,** including supermarkets, are generally open 9am to 6pm while restaurants, cinemas and other entertainment stay open until 11pm. Outside of the cities, smaller malls close on Sundays.

There are **markets** all over the country selling crafts, clothing, gifts and food. These are usually held at the weekends from 9am to 4pm and many are worth a trip (even if you do not want to buy anything) as they offer numerous activities and entertainment.

Payment
Almost all shops take **credit cards**, although Visa and MasterCard are far more widely accepted than other brands. In markets and smaller shops you'll need cash. International visitors can **reclaim the 14 per cent VAT** on all purchases taken out of the country. This is done at the airport on departure and you will need to show your passport and air ticket as well as VAT receipts of purchases. Visit www.taxrefunds.co.za for more information.

What to Buy
African crafts, art and curios such as wooden or tin sculptures, masks, cloth and beaded jewellery from countries all over the continent can be found in South Africa. Look out for items made by local people. **Fashion** is comparable to Europe and North America and there are a number of quality chain stores and shops.

South Africa is well known for its **wine**, and the ideal place to purchase wine is in the Cape Winelands.

Taking home wildlife souvenirs sourced from rare or endangered species is highly unethical as it encourages poaching. In addition, it is likely to be illegal in your home country.

CALENDER OF EVENTS

South Africans love to celebrate but not all local festivals or events will appeal to foreign visitors.

In addition to famous events, such as the Hermanus Whale Festival or the Cape Town Jazz Festival, there are also many smaller events. These events celebrate regional cultures, street art and South African music styles (such as Kwaito).

And there are also various culinary events, such as the Knysna Oyster Festival. When the celebrations are underway you should remember to pay special attention to your valuables. It is best to leave all your valuables in the hotel safe.

The following is a small selection of the most important festivals and events:

JANUARY TO MARCH

Clarens Craft Beer Festival
The festival takes place in the Free State at the end of February and showcases over 70 different craft beers.
www.clarenscraftbeerfest.com

Cape Town Jazz Festival
All the jazz greats rendezvous in Cape Town at the end of March.
www.capetownjazzfest.com

Splashy Fen Music Festival
At around Easter, South Africa's largest music festival draws the stars of the local and international scene to a farm near Underberg in KwaZulu-Natal where revellers celebrate around the clock.
www.splashyfen.co.za

APRIL, MAY

Pink Loerie Mardi Gras
At the end of April/beginning of May, the gay and lesbian community take over the streets of tranquil Knysna and celebrate gay pride with a vibrant Mardi Gras.
www.pinkloerie.co.za

Riebeek Valley Olive Festival
In early May, the Western Cape's olive farmers celebrate a successful harvest with a culinary festival that includes live entertainment, games, olive products and – of course – lots of olive oil tastings.
https://riebeekvalleyolivefestival.co.za

JUNE, JULY

National Arts Festival
At the end of June/beginning of July, Grahamstown hosts an ambitious arts festival with theatre productions, music concerts and dance performances by South African artists.
www.nationalartsfestival.co.za

Knysna Oyster Festival
At the beginning of July, the Knysna festival showcases local oysters along with other culinary delights, wine-tasting and music events.
www.oysterfestival.co.za

SEPTEMBER, OCTOBER

Arts Alive
In September, Johannesburg celebrates the African roots of jazz, hip-hop, R&B, house and Afropop, there are also poetry and dance performances and panel discussions.
www.arts-alive.co.za

Joy of Jazz Festival
At the end of September, Johannesburg draws all the jazz greats for its flagship, multi-stage festive.
www.joyofjazz.co.za

Hermanus Whale Festival
At the end of September/beginning of October, Hermanus (and the town's Whale Crier) celebrate the whale-watching season with a festival of food, drink and music.
http://hermanuswhalefestival.co.za

Oppikoppi Bushveld Festival
In October, the Northwest Province hosts South African's version of Glastonbury, with country's largest rock, pop, and indie festival. What began on a small farm today draws tens of thousands visitors.
www.oppikoppi.co.za

USEFUL WORDS AND PHRASES

South Africa has 11 official languages: Sepedi, Sesotho, Setswana, siSwati, Tshivenda, Xitsonga, Afrikaans, English, isiNdebele, isiXhosa and isiZulu. English is generally spoken by everyone but a simple hello or thank you in the local language of the region you're travelling through goes a long way.

After English, the three most commonly used languages are Afrikaans (countrywide), isiZulu (predominantly KwaZulu-Natal) and isiXhosa (predominantly Eastern Cape). Speakers of these also live in the large cities. All are generally spoken as they are written, though isiXhosa and isiZulu have letters that are represented by various "clicks" – made by slapping the tongue against various parts of the inside of the mouth.

Getting Started

I'm just a beginner at isiZulu	**Ngisaqala ukufunda isiZulu**
I only speak a little Xhosa	**Ndithetha isiXhosa kancinci nje**
I am trying to learn Afrikaans, but I cannot speak it yet	**Ek probeer tans Afrikaans leer, maar ek kan dit nog nie praat nie**

Useful Words in Afrikaans

Afternoon	**Middag**		Ice cream	**Roomys**
Airplane	**Vliegtuig**		Information	**Inligting**
Airport	**Lughawe**		Left	**Links**
Arrival	**Aankoms**		Low-lying lake/ swamp	**Vlei**
Bank	**Bank**		Lunch	**Middagete**
Barbecue	**Braai**		Market	**Mark**
Bed-and- breakfast	**Bed en ontbyt**		Menu	**Spyskaart**
Beach	**Strand**		Milk	**Melk**
Bill	**Rekening**		Morning	**Oggend**
Border	**Grens**		Night	**Nag**
Borough	**Burg**		Petrol	**Brandstoff**
Bread	**Brood**		Pharmacy	**Apteek**
Breakfast	**Ontbyt**		Police	**Polisie**
Cheap	**Goedkoop**		Post office	**Poskantoor**
Cheque	**Tjek**		Pub/bar	**Kroeg**
Chips	**Skyfies**		Right	**Regs**
Church	**Kerk**		Sausage	**(Boere)wors**
City	**Stad**		Station	**Stasie**
Credit card	**Kredietkaart**		Ticket	**Kaartjie**
Departure	**Vertrek**		Today	**Vandag**
Dinner	**Aandete**		Tomorrow	**Môre**
Evening	**Aand**		Town centre	**Middestad**
Expensive	**Duur**		Traveller's cheque	**Reisigerstjek**
Exit	**Uitgang**		Village	**Dorp**
Field	**Veld**		Wine	**Wyn**
Good/nice	**Lekker**		Yesterday	**Gister**

Useful Phrases

ENGLISH	ISIZULU	ISIXHOSA	AFRIKAANS
Hello	Sawubona	Uphila njani?	Hallo
How are you?	Kunjani?	Uphila njani?	Hoe gaan dit?
Fine, thanks	Ngiyaphila	Ndiphilile, enkosi	Goed dankie
Yes / No	Yebo / Cha	Ewe / Cha	Ja / Nee
Please	Ngiyakucela	Nceda	Asseblief
Thank you	Ngiyabonga	Enkosi	Baie dankie
Excuse me	Uxolo	Uxolo	Verskoon my
What is your name?	Ngubani igama lakho?	Ngubani igama lakho?	Wit is jou naam?
My name is...	Igama lami ngu...	Igama lam ngu...	My naam is ...
Where do you live?	Uhlalaphi?	Uhlala phi?	Waar woon jy?
I come from...	Ngiphuma e...	Ndivela...	Ek kom vanaf...
How much is it?	Kuyimalini lokhu?	Ixabisa malini?	Hoeveel kos dit?
Where is...?	Ihpi ...?	Ihpi ...?	Waar is ...?
What is this/that?	Yintoni le/leyo?	Yini le/leyo?	Wat is dit/daardie?
I would like...	Ngifuna...	Ndingathanda...	Ek wil graag...hê
What time is it?	Yisikhathisini manje?	Ngubani ixesha?	Hoe laat is dit?
I am looking for...	Ngifuna i...	Ndikhangela i...	Ek is opsoek na die...
I am sorry	Ngiyaxolisa	Ndiva mtoembi	Ek is jammer
I don't know	Angazi	Andazi	Ek weet nie
I don't understand	Andiqondi	Andiqondi	Ek verstaan nie
Do you speak English?	Uyakwazi ukukhuluma isiNgisi?	Uyakwazi ukuthetha isiNgesi?	Praat jy Engels?
See you later	Sizobonana	Sobe sibonane	Sien jou later
Goodbye	Uhambe kahle/ Usale kahle	Sala sentle	Totsiens

Numbers

	ISIZULU	ISIXHOSA	AFRIKAANS
1	ukunye	nye	een
2	isibili	mbini	twee
3	kuthathu	ntathu	drie
4	okune	ne	vier
5	isihlanu	ntlanu	vyf
6	isithupha	ntandathu	ses
7	isikhombisa	xhenxe	sewe
8	isishiyagalombili	bhozo	agt
9	isishiyagalolunye	lithoba	nege
10	ishumi	lishuymi	tien
11	ishumi nanye	ishumi elinanye	elf
12	ishumi nambili	ishumi elinesibini	twaalf
13	ishumi nantathu	ishumi elinesithathu	dertien
14	ishumi nane	elinesine	veertien
15	ishumi nesihlanu	elinesihlanu	vyftien
20	amashumi amabili	amashumi amabini	twintig
50	amashumi amahlanu	amashumi amahlanu	vyftig
100	ikhulu	ikhulu	(een) honderd
1,000	inkulungwane	iwaka	(een) duisend

Road Atlas

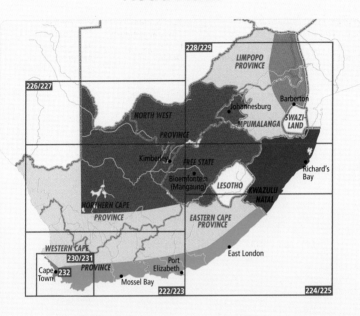

Key to Road Atlas

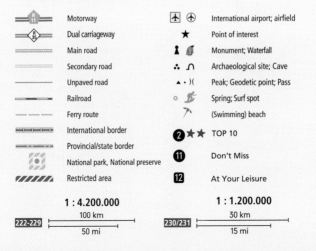

Motorway	✈ ⊕	International airport; airfield
Dual carriageway	★	Point of interest
Main road	⚑ ⋔	Monument; Waterfall
Secondary road	⁙ ∩	Archaeological site; Cave
Unpaved road	▲ ·)(	Peak; Geodetic point; Pass
Railroad	○ 🏄	Spring; Surf spot
Ferry route	↗	(Swimming) beach
International border	② ★★	TOP 10
Provincial/state border	⑪	Don't Miss
National park, National preserve	⑫	At Your Leisure
Restricted area		

1 : 4.200.000	1 : 1.200.000
100 km	30 km
222-229	230/231
50 mi	15 mi

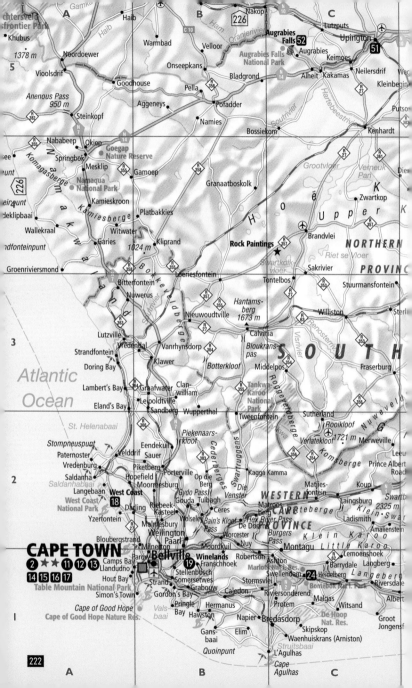

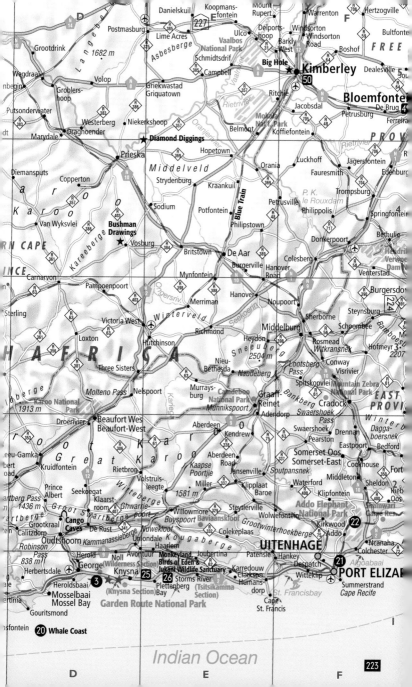

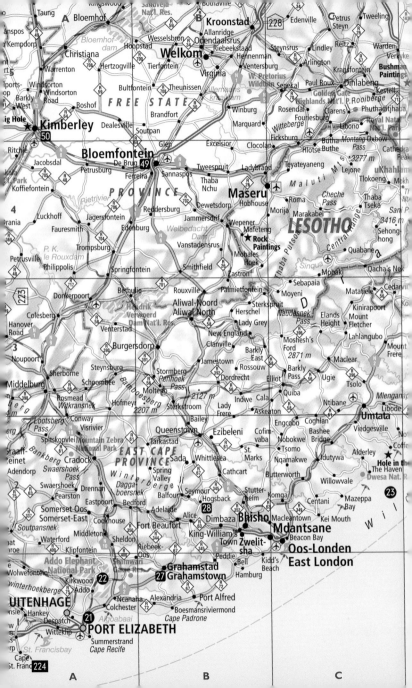

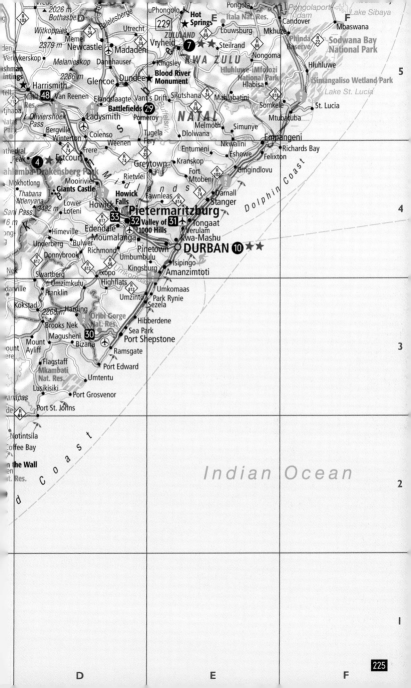

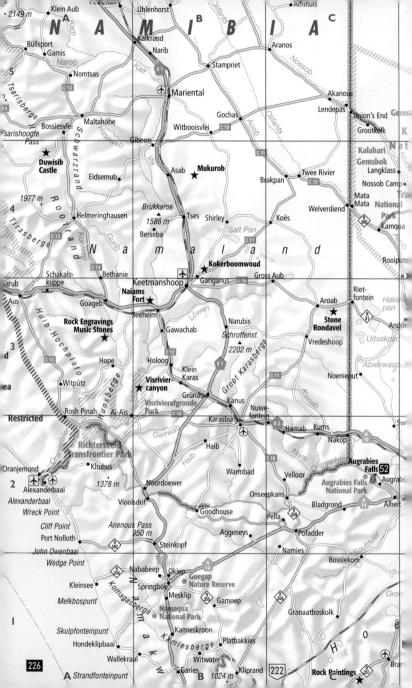

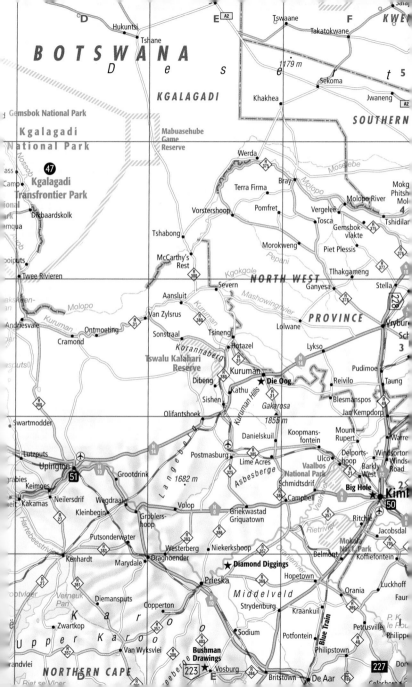

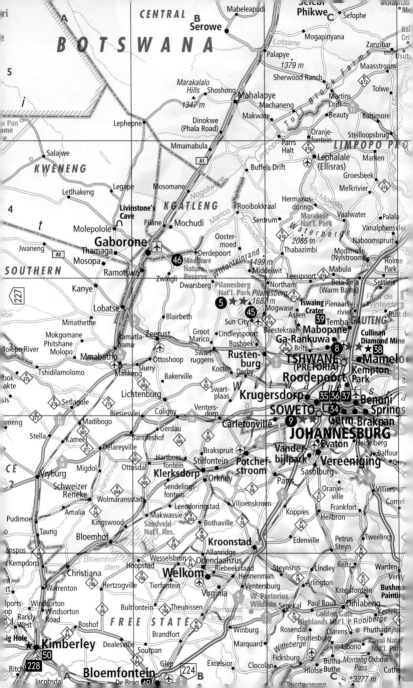

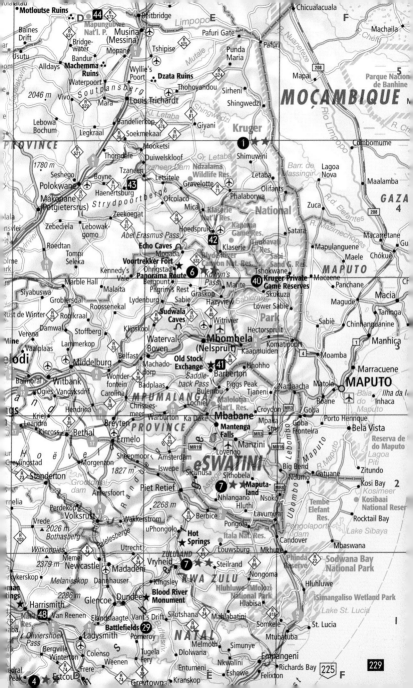

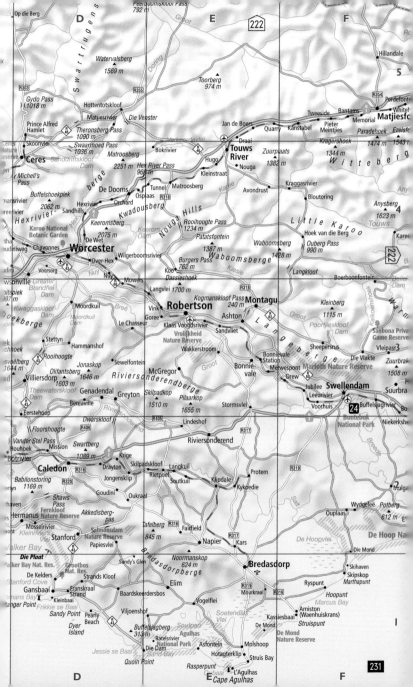

Cape Town

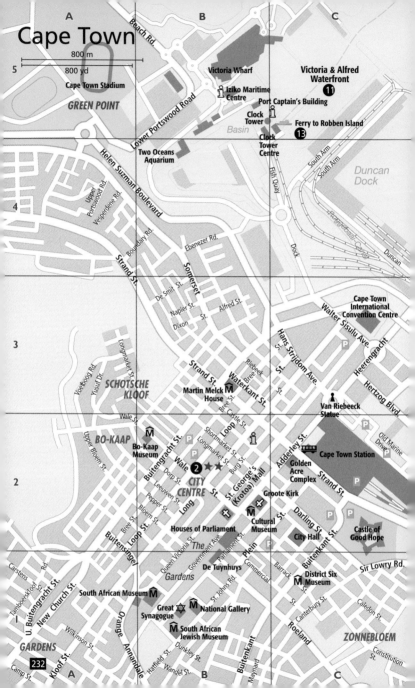

800 m
800 yd

A

B

C

5

Cape Town Stadium

GREEN POINT

Beach Rd.

Victoria Wharf

Iziko Maritime Centre

Victoria & Alfred Waterfront ⑪

Port Captain's Building

Clock Tower

Ferry to Robben Island ⑬

Lower Portswood Road

Clock Tower Centre

Basin

Two Oceans Aquarium

Fish Quay

Duncan Dock

South Arm

South Arm

Dock

Duncan

4

Helen Suzman Boulevard

Upper Portswood Rd.

Vesperdene Rd.

Boundary Rd.

Strand St.

Ebenezer Rd.

Somerset

De Smit St.

Napier St.

Dixon St.

Alfred St.

Cape Town International Convention Centre

Walter Sisulu Ave.

Heerengracht

Hertzog Blvd.

3

SCHOTSCHE KLOOF

Longmarket St.

Voetboog Rd.

Yusuf Dr.

Strand St.

Waterkant St.

Riebeeck St.

Bree St.

Hans Strijdom Ave.

Martin Melck House Ⓜ

Bree St.

Van Riebeeck Statue

Old Marine Drive

BO-KAAP

Wale St.

Ⓜ

Bo-Kaap Museum

Upper Bloem St.

Buitengracht St.

Longmarket St.

Shortmarket St.

Loop St.

Burg St.

Cape Town Station

Adderley St.

Golden Acre Complex

Strand St.

2

CITY CENTRE

Dorp St.

Leeuwen St.

Pepper St.

Bloem St.

Bree St.

Loop St.

Long St.

Wale St.

② ★★

St. George's (Krotoa) Mall

Groote Kirk

Darling St.

Castle of Good Hope

Buitenkant St.

Houses of Parliament

Queen Victoria St.

Government Ave.

The Gardens

St. Johns Rd.

Plein St.

Parliament St.

Commercial St.

Cultural Museum Ⓜ

City Hall

Barrack St.

De Tuynhuys

District Six Museum Ⓜ

Sir Lowry Rd.

Carstens St.

U. Buitengracht St.

New Church St.

Tamboerskloof St.

Kloof St.

Wilkinson St.

Orange St.

Annandale

South African Museum Ⓜ

Great Synagogue ✡

National Gallery Ⓜ

South African Jewish Museum Ⓜ

Buitenkant St.

Canterbury St.

Caledon St.

Roeland St.

ZONNEBLOEM

GARDENS

Camp St.

Hatfield St.

Dunkley St.

Wandel St.

Maynard St.

Constitution St.

232

Index